Sandhurst 6/02.

YESTERDAY'S TOWN: BURNHAM

High Street, Burnham c1900, when the Swan Hotel was a centre for social activities. (BS)

*St Peter's Church, Burnham, from a painting by Florence Stocker,
c1885. (BS)*

YESTERDAY'S TOWN:
BURNHAM

BY

DOROTHY BLACKMAN DAPHNE CHEVOUS
MERVYN EDEN ANTHONY PACKE AND
OLIVER SPENCER

BARRACUDA BOOKS LIMITED
BUCKINGHAM, ENGLAND
MCMLXXXIV

PUBLISHED IN 1984 BY BARRACUDA BOOKS LIMITED
BUCKINGHAM, ENGLAND
AND PRINTED
IN THIS SECOND EDITION IN 1988 BY
M. & A. THOMSON LITHO LIMITED
GLASGOW, SCOTLAND

BOUND BY
WOOLNOUGH BOOKBINDING LIMITED
IRTHLINGBOROUGH, ENGLAND

JACKET PRINTED BY
CHENEY & SONS LIMITED
BANBURY, OXON

LITHOGRAPHY BY
SOUTH MIDLANDS LITHOPLATES LIMITED
LUTON, ENGLAND

DISPLAY SET IN TIMES
AND TEXT SET IN 12/13 TIMES ROMAN BY
BEDFORDSHIRE GRAPHICS LIMITED
BEDFORD, ENGLAND

CORRECTIONS BY KEY COMPOSITION
NORTHAMPTON, ENGLAND

© Dorothy Blackman 1984 & 1988

ISBN 0 86023 435 5

CONTENTS

Dedication
For the people of Burnham.

ACKNOWLEDGEMENTS

A book of this kind can only be produced with a great deal of assistance and co-operation from others. We have been so overwhelmed with help from so many people, that this book has become almost a community project and it is impossible to mention everyone by name. Some however must be acknowledged for, without their assistance, this book would never have been completed.

We thank Caroline Gillies for producing a large collection of old photographs and the Burnham Society for consent for us to draw extensively upon it; the Bucks County Record Office and the *Windsor Slough & Eton Express*, for permission to reproduce items from their archives, and the *Slough Observer* for photocopies of their newspapers; Burnham and Farnham Common Librarians and Paul Sherriff, who acted as subscriber reception centres; Joan Spencer and Mary Bentley for help with the research; Ruth Ibbotson for use of her map analysis; David Webb, who reproduced many of the pictures; Joan Handley, Muriel Hayns and Mary Haskell for assistance with typing; Jim Isaac, Fred Jaycock and Oliver Watts, for their longevity and wonderful memories, and the many people who willingly lent their precious photographs; and finally, thanks are due from the rest of the Group to Tony Packe who, years ago, salvaged so much information from the past, which might otherwise have been lost forever.

KEY TO CAPTION CREDITS

AE	Mrs A. Evans	GM	Godfrey Moon
AS	Alfred Sands	GS	Mrs G. Skinner
BA	Mrs B. Adaway	JH	Mrs J. Handley
BBC	Burnham Bowls Club	JPH	John P. Hall
BCC	Burnham Cricket Club	JT	Jim Taylor
BC/CRO	Bucks County Record Office	KL	Mrs K. Lilley
BS	The Burnham Society	KT	Ken Trimming
BFC	Burnham Football Club	LA	Mrs L. Allder
BRC	Burnham Rifle Club	LR	Laurie Reynolds
CC	Cyril Cox	MC	Miss M. Collett
CUL	Cambridge University Library	ME	Mervyn Eden
DD	Daniel Davis	MEC	Miss M.E. Cleare
DH	Desmond Hayns	MJ	Mrs M. Jaycock
DSB	Mrs D.S. Blackman	NT	Nancy Treleaven
DW	Doreen Wootton	OB	Olive Bird
EH	Mrs E. Holloway	OW	Oliver Watts
EM	Miss E. Mitchell	PC	Phyllis Crumplin
EP	Mrs E. Parrett	RA	Roy Almond
FBC	Mrs F.B. Cleare	RI	Ruth Ibbotson
FJ	Frank Jackson	RM	Rev Mother (House of Prayer)
FP	Mrs F. Packe	SPB	St Peter's Belfry
FW	Father Woodard	WC	William Cox
GL	Gordon Limmer	WM	Mrs W. Miles

INTRODUCTION

The dusty High Street of a century ago, with cartwheels grinding over the stones, the clip-clop of horses' hooves, girls skipping, chanting rhymes with their ropes strung across the street, the hiss of red-hot iron as the blacksmith shod horses by the roadside and the lowing of cattle on their way to the slaughterhouse, is a far cry from the car-lined street and modern shop fronts of today. Old cottages huddled between the shops have given place to offices, and the once residential High Street is now busy with shoppers and workers by day, but deserted at night.

It is this ever-hastening change which prompted the authors to put together the fruits of their researches, and pictures and memories of those who can recall the old ways, before they are gone forever. We have tried thus to provide a factual and accurate record of events and changes that have taken place over nearly two centuries. Pigot's Directory in the early 1800s described Burnham as a place of great antiquity, but of no particular note except for the scenery and views. This may have seemed so to visitors, but to the people of Burnham the village had much to commend it. To them it was home — either the home of their family for generations, or the place they had chosen to settle in, to live, work and bring up their families in, and whatever position in life they aspired to, each class of society had its place within the community. It was largely a self-supporting and mutually supportive society where charity was a necessary benevolence between rich and poor.

The Parish Church of St Peter was the focal point of administration then, when the Vicar, local gentry and the wealthier traders subscribed money and initiated any improvements in the village. This ensured them as benefactors, and the local traders and craftsmen benefitted from supplying materials and providing the workforce for public buildings and improvements. This method of administration was the forerunner of Parish Councils.

Drawn together by a mutual interest in discovering and preserving the past of our village, Burnham Historians have enjoyed writing this book, and wish to thank all those who have contributed to it. With the need for economy in words, it was not possible to include all the information available — but another book, another time. Where possible, names and dates are included in the picture captions and, if readers can provide further names, we shall be pleased to hear from them.

We hope this book may prove a source of information and pleasure.

Dorothy Blackman *Daphne Chevous*

Mervyn Eden *attachue* *OB Spencer*

PROLOGUE

At the time of the Domesday Book the Manor of Burnham was held by Walter Fitz-Otho, and comprised eighteen hides of land, woodland for 600 swine, and was worth £10.

The Manor passed down the family of Fitz-Otho to William, who took the surname de Windsor, the family also being Castellans of Windsor Castle. In 1204 William's heir Walter divided the estate between Duncan de Lascelles and Ralph Hodeng. De Lascelles' son Thomas transferred his portion to Richard, Earl of Cornwall c1230, while Ralph Hodeng's grandson left his estate to his aunt, who was married to Sir William de Huntercombe. Their son Thomas was constable of Windsor Castle, and his son John, inheriting in 1327, built the present house at Huntercombe of which the mediaeval hall still remains. It was then known as the Manor of Burnham alias Huntercombe.

In 1265 Richard, Earl of Cornwall, founded Burnham Abbey and endowed it with his part of the Manor of Burnham. The Abbess was granted the right to hold a market in the village every Thursday and a Fair on the festival of St Matthew. She was also granted Aymill, a water mill south-east of Burnham Village, from which a stream ran through Cippenham and the grounds of Burnham Abbey to the Thames at Dorney. In 1395 the Abbess was cited at Cippenham Manor Court for stopping the flow of water in Aymill Brook, allowing it to overflow the tenants' lands. She was fined 2s.

At this time the main road from London to Bath passed through Burnham. When the road was diverted to its present course, Burnham lost its market, which was transferred to Maidenhead, although a 16th century Market Hall in Church Street existed until about 1940.

In 1368, on the death of John of Huntercombe's grandson, an enquiry was held, attended among others by John, the clerk of Burnham. They swore an oath that 'John of Huntercombe' held the Manor of Burnham, which consisted of 150 acres of arable, 12 acres of pasture, 10 acres of meadow and six acres of wood and scrub.

The next heir (the fourth John) died childless and the male line of Huntercombe came to an end in 1390; the Manor passed to an aunt married to Philip Skydmore of Herefordshire. Their son George Skydmore in 1430 collected £3 rental fees from Burnham, including 4s 8d from the Manor of Poyle, and 2s for Stompe Hyll. Tenants included John Alderygge, Walter Aleyn, Thomas Ballard, William Wodeward, John Lee, John Gregory, William Walter, John Hyll and John Lewyn.

A complaint was made to the Archdeacon in 1521 that the Vicar of Burnham, John Mallet, had kept horses and dogs in the Church.

At this time a school was held in the Abbey for girls up to 14 years and boys up to 8 years. Four children, one of whom was Michael Bovington, were attending in 1521. But the days of the Abbey were numbered. In 1533 Henry VIII declared himself Head of the Church in England and, in 1534, Margaret Gibson, the Abbess of Burnham, 'submitted unwillingly' to the Act of Supremacy. She resigned soon

afterwards, but her successor Alys Baldwin and the nine nuns signed the Deed of Dissolution in 1539.

The Lordship of the Manor was retained by the Crown but in 1631 it was amalgamated with the Manor of Huntercombe. The lands were leased by the Crown to William Tyldesley, who inherited some of the Abbess's rights, though his rent for Aymill doubled, as he was using it for brewing. The next tenant, Paul Wentworth, who married Tyldesley's widow, granted a lease to the miller, John Lidgold, reserving for himself the mill-pond and fish and the use of the pond for keeping swans and breeding cygnets. Part of the miller's job was to keep the brook from the mill clean. He neglected his duty and was turned out, because Wentworth's house was not kept 'sweet and clean from annoyance of foul water'.

Before enclosure the farmland consisted of three large fields; Tockley to the north, Britwell to the east, and Lent to the South of the main street. There was no Enclosure Act for Burnham, the fields being enclosed piecemeal by agreement among those concerned. The common land was to the north of the village, comprising what is now the Gore, and stretching northwards for several miles, until some part was enclosed by Lord Grenville when he began building his estate at Dropmore in 1792.

In 1542 Vicar John Mallet had forfeited his life for speaking against the dissolution of the monasteries, and the King became patron of the living. He presented Richard Davis but, with the accession of Catholic Queen Mary in 1553, Davis lost the living because he was married, returning in 1559 under Elizabeth I.

The Skydmore line at Huntercombe ended in 1606, when the third Philip Skydmore sold the estate and manorial rights to Sir Marmaduke Darrell. This was the end of the family line of Walter Fitz-Otho. The Civil War was approaching and the Darrells were loyal to the King. In the year that Charles I was executed, Huntercombe was alienated by Parliament and sold to one of its supporters, George Evelyn, Captain of a troop of horse. The Evelyn Memorial in Burnham Church shows him with his wife and two sons.

Cromwell's soldiers were quartered in Burnham during the Civil War. In December 1645 Lieutenant Ryder and his troopers were 'found typpling' in Burnham, and refused to pursue a party of Royalists who had carried off men and horses from Cippenham. For many years it was believed that Cromwell's troops pollarded trees in the Beeches, but this is now thought to be due to the villagers' rights to 'lop and top' for firewood. The woodland was more extensive at that time than now.

Diarist John Evelyn described his cousin's house at Huntercombe as '- - a pretty seat in the forest'. In 1672 this estate comprised three messuages, seven orchards, seven gardens, 10 cottages, one dovehouse, 340 acres of land, 40 acres of meadow, 20 acres of furze and heath, £3 10s 0d in rent, and also the Courts Leet (criminal) and Baron (land tenure). George Evelyn's grandson and heir, William, was baptised in Burnham Church on 4 October 1667. He later sold the Manor to Thomas Eyre of Allerds, Lord of the Manor of East Burnham, with which Burnham Manor now became amalgamated. In 1786 Charles Eyre left the Manor to his nephew Captain Henry Sayer, who in turn left it to Charles Eyre's son-in-law John Popple.

That brings this brief history to the beginning of the book.

YESTERDAY'S TOWN

ABOVE: A typical scene in Burnham Beeches; BELOW: High Street looking north, showing the dome-topped telephone exchange built 1930, after the Britwell exchange closed.

ABOVE: Looking eastwards into Lincoln Hatch Lane with the Priory wall on the right, c1915; (EM) BELOW: Britwell Road looking towards the Crispin, c1920.

OPPOSITE ABOVE: The junction with Court Lane, after Britwell Road was diverted to the North of Upper Britwell Farm; CENTRE: the Gore, showing to the left, the cottages, formerly the Gore School. BELOW: Britwell Road and Green Lane crossroads leading to the Golf Course and the Beeches. LEFT: Dawes East Path looking west, with Miss Winch's cottage at the end on the left by the 'kissing gate'. (EM) RIGHT: Mrs Winch at a window of the family cottage in Dawes East Lane c1885, now demolished, (BS) and BELOW: the Winch family in their front garden in Dawes East Lane c1885. The cottage next door is now demolished. (BS)

15

Emma Blackman with her brood c1902. Born in Alma Row in 1869 she lived there until her death in 1947. (DSB)

*ABOVE: Haymill Pond, showing the sluice gates, (BS) and
BELOW: from a painting by J. Herbert Snell, c1895. (BS)*

ABOVE: Adam and Eve Lane at the junction with Dropmore Road, (EM) and BELOW: the Old Thatched Cottage at Lent Green, c1920.

18

ABOVE: Lent Rise Road looking north, with Trimming's Garage, the first in Burnham, with petrol pumps outside, c1915; CENTRE: when the High Street was still largely residential. Tudor cottages, left, and bay windowed house, centre right, before the wooden shop facia added in 1903 as Rhys-Williams' chemist's; (BS) LEFT: the Tudor cottages opposite the foundry prior to demolition in 1923; (BS) RIGHT: the old Red Lion, demolished c1940 to make way for the present pub. (GL)

19

ABOVE LEFT: High Street looking north c1920. Mr Cleare's house opposite the Crispin, the Alma pub in the distance; most of the right hand shops are now demolished; RIGHT: Church Street c1910: the slaughterhouse through the gap between the buildings; (RA) CENTRE: before the Old Five Bells had its first face-lift. Next door was the headmaster's house and Tudor Cottage, right, was a shop, c1900; (BS) BELOW LEFT: in the opposite direction with the vicarage in the distance, the school at the end and the 16th century Market House, now gone, bearing the dates 1271-1539, and RIGHT: the Old Five Bells after a face-lift, when 5 bells were moulded in relief, c1920. (BS)

ABOVE: High Street in 1923 with Whiteley's dress shop left and Sands' Old Brewery Garage, right and BELOW: the timbered building, formerly gabled, is early 16th century. The cart is by Jarratt's, c1920. (BS)

BURNHAM (5,000), Bucks. [*Map* 8.C.2.] London 23¾ miles.

L.H. 10–2, 6–10 w.d.; 12–2, 7–10 S. E. Closing—Thurs. Post—6.0 p.m.
Ten Mile Speed Limit.
High Wycombe 8½, Beaconsfield 5☐ Burnham Beeches 2, Farnham Common 3☐
Slough 3, Eton 4½, Windsor 5☐ Maidenhead 3½☐.

HOTEL.

✶   **Swan**; 3 brms.; S.R. 3/–; D.R. 5/–; B. 3/–; L. to order; L.c. 2/6;
L.h. 3/6; T. 1/6; H.T. 2/6; D. to order 4/–; Pub. G. adj.

GARAGE.

✶✶   **W. J. Sands**, Old Brewery Garage, High Street; T.A., Sands; T.N., 85;
G.A.—C. 50; M/C. 12; L.u. 3; O.N. at call; O.S.; C.h.; M/C. & R.; B.E.

BURNHAM BEECHES (4,113), Bucks. [*Map* 8.C.2.] London
25½ miles.

L.H. 10–2, 6–10 w.d.; 12–2, 7–10 S. E. Closing—Thurs. Post—7.20 p.m.
Bourne End 5, Beaconsfield 4, Farnham Common ½☐ Slough 4½, Eton 6, Windsor 6½☐
Burnham 2, High Wycombe 8☐.

HOTEL.

✶   **Grenville Lodge** (Unlic.); T.N., Farnham Common 227; 4 brms.; S.R.
2/6 to 6/6; D.R. 5/6 to 7/6; B. 2/6; L. in season; L.c. 2/6; L.h. 3/6; T. 1/6;
H.T. 2/6; D. to order; Ch. 7/6; G.A.—L.u. 4; f.d.m.; 1/6 to 2/– N.

OPPOSITE ABOVE: About 1920, showing the Council Rooms and Library at the corner of Church Street by the lamp post; (BS) CENTRE LEFT: Mrs Watts outside her cottage in Church Street c1930; formerly the Bricklayers Arms; (BS) RIGHT: Tile House, left, on the site of the 'lock-up'. The garden wall next to it is all that remains of the Bricklayers Arms, Church Street. c1950. (BS) BELOW LEFT: Swan Cottage, Brewery House and Brewery, right, are 16th and 17th century, with 'Kevoch' where Harry Baldwin lived beyond, c1910; (BS) RIGHT: an artist's impression of the Market Hall in Church Street. (BS) ABOVE: When the Swan Hotel charged 5s for a double room and Sands' was still called the Old Brewery Garage, 1929, and BELOW: Cleare's butcher's left, (now Frost's), opposite Harry Baldwin's house and Hebbes the cornmerchant, c1900. (BS)

22

THE OLD MARKET HALL,
BURNHAM
NOW DEMOLISHED.

ABOVE: A horse being shod at Lloyd's farriers next to the Rose and Crown, c1910, (BS) and BELOW: the butcher surveys the scene from outside Hall's shop while a lady 'cycles unperturbed on the wrong side of the street, c1910. (BS)

ABOVE: The War Memorial with the infant school, left, before the Working Men's Club front hedge, right, was removed, c1925, and BELOW: gypsies in Burnham Beeches: they gave donkey rides, c1915. (EM)

AT HOME ON THE LAND

In the 18th century the parish of Burnham consisted of six Liberties: Town and Wood, Cippenham, East Burnham, Britwell, and Upper and Lower Boveney. The principal landowners were the Eyre family who, until 1786, were Lords of the Manor of Allerds and later also of Huntercombe. The manor house at East Burnham was demolished in 1837. Arabella, one of the last Eyres, married Lieutenant John Popple of the 11th Dragoons, who had become an important landowner in the east and south of the parish before his death in 1831.

John Popple was succeeded as primary landowner by William Wyndham Grenville, son of George Grenville and Elizabeth Wyndham. Born in 1759, educated at Eton and Oxford, he became MP for Buckingham in 1782, Speaker of the House of Commons in 1789, and on the first day of the new Parliament in 1790 was created Baron Grenville of Wotton-under-Bernwood, Bucks. He married Anne, a niece of William Pitt, in 1792. Foreign Secretary from 1791 to 1801, he was Prime Minister in 1806-7.

His eldest brother George, Marquis of Buckingham, bought the reversion of a six acre property at Littleworth Common called Dropmore Lodge from a Mr Gordon, an indirect descendant of the Eyre family, and transferred it to William, who then acquired land in the north of the parish. A large area of common land there had become less important in the rural economy as a result of the recent enclosures, so Lord Grenville could enlarge his estate easily, rehousing some tenants and rerouting roads around it. The cottage was replaced by a mansion, which had an excellent view to and from Windsor Castle, once an intervening hill had been lowered. An artificial hill formed of tree stumps and gravel, called Root Hill or Stump Hill, offered views as far as Harrow. After the roads near the house were diverted, the estate enjoyed much more privacy, and landscaping included one of the earliest arboreta in the country, covering some six hundred acres. A subterranean ice-house was filled every winter with ice from the estate ponds and then packed with hay as insulation. In 1810 a bargeload of soot was delivered via Hedsor for the gardens and, by 1819, the House, stables and greenhouses were insured for £13,800 with a further £3,000 for the contents.

Burnham was primarily a farming area. In the years of depression during and after the Napoleonic Wars, the former three Fairs a year had declined to one annual Fair, primarily for hiring servants on 1 and 2 October. In 1813 the Fair embraced horses, cattle, sheep and hog dealing; the High Street brewery needed barley, and other crops sold then included wheat, oats, kidney beans, peas, potatoes, clover and meadow grass.

Farmers were concerned about access and damage to their lands: in 1812 damage done by the Berkley Hunt was such that, when the magistrates met in the Swan, those aggrieved by the Hunt were meeting at the George. In 1817 William Bayley, Edmund Mason and John Agar issued notices threatening prosecution of those sporting on their lands.

Farm labourers' and estate workers' wages were 11s to 14s a week in 1834; most of them stayed with one employer for long periods, for there was little scope for additional income. Few labourers owned their own cottages; some sought more money; for example old Mr Avenal of Dropmore Lodge played the melodion and fiddle outside the Feathers at Cliveden. The women worked in the market gardens, during harvest, and in the north-east of the parish at pillow lacemaking. In 1885 young Edith Avenal used to collect water for an old lady from a distant tap, and took her father's lunch of a home-made cottage loaf filled with bacon or eggs to him in the fields.

In the town itself many cottages were owned by the gentry and by leading farmers, who let them to their labourers. Owners of land surrounding the town in 1839 included Elizabeth Vaughan, Ann Boncey, Richard Cleare, Benjamin Baldwin, John Winch, Philip Frost, William Bayley, and Richard Boncey, former owner of the iron foundry. In the Tithe returns for that year four landowners held half the parish lands between them: Lady Grenville, who held most (29%), William Bayley junior, John Pocock and Edmund Brown of Cippenham Place. Many local properties changed hands then; between 1815 and 1822 Horse Harness, Allerds, Lake End, Britwell and Poyle Farms and The Grove and Britwell Court were offered for sale.

Britwell Court dates back to the 14th century, though the block including the main entrance, the oldest remaining section, is from the 16th century. It was owned in the 18th century by Charles Boyle, Earl of Orrery and a patron of the maker of the first orrery, followed by Crayle Crayle and around 1794 by Anne Lady Ravensworth, a local benefactress. The 19th century brought Lord Boston, whose family name was Irby; he lived there until his death in 1822. He also had properties in Hitcham and Hedsor and had joined Lord Grenville in opposing a Bill to build a canal across the area from Maidenhead to Hillingdon. The house then became a small pre-Eton preparatory school run by Rev Dr Evans, whose son Sir John Evans was a well-known archaeologist. It was purchased by William Henry Miller in 1830, the year in which he became MP for Newcastle under Lyme; an eminent book collector, his new home housed the Britwell Library.

Meanwhile Lord Grenville acquired more land and property, including Huntercombe Manor in 1812. He may well have purchased Huntercombe solely for the magnificent wrought iron gates, which he transferred to Dropmore, where they remain today, and he lived there until his death in 1834. His sister, Elizabeth, who became Lady Wells, lived at Huntercombe Manor from 1812 to 1842, during when Lord Grenville planted the two magnificent magnolias on the south side, and the great Venetian sumach tree. Daughter of the Earl of Carysfort, Elizabeth took a particular interest in Cippenham, made a bequest in support of the village school there and was buried in the Grenville vaults at St Peter's church with other members of that family.

On Henry Miller's death in 1848, Britwell Court passed successively to Misses Sarah and Ellen Marsh. Miller intended to bequeath the Library to the Bodleian at Oxford, but Ellen Marsh, by a codicil to her will in 1861, left it with the house to one

of Miller's relations, Samuel Christy MP, who took the name of Christie-Miller by Royal Licence in 1862. He built a special fireproof room with an elementary sprinkler system as a further safeguard to house the Library. Further from the village centre on the southern edge of Burnham Common was East Burnham Park, a house where George Grote lived from 1838 to 1852; author of an eight-volume History of Greece and one of the founders of London University in the 1820s, he nicknamed his new Elizabethan-style country house the 'History Hut', since it was built from the proceeds of his book.

The Priory was built c1824, to the south of Burnham High Street, and had a succession of owners and occupiers, though not until 1887 did the house and its owner (then Captain Farwell) play a significant part in village life. The annual ploughing match, inaugurated in 1835, took place on the bigger farms, such as Austin and Tombs' land in 1843 when 26 teams entered, each ploughing ½ an acre. Afterwards 40 farmers and tradesmen dined at the George, while about 90 servants consumed a roast beef and plum pudding meal in various public houses. The church bells rang throughout the day.

When the Tithe map and schedule were prepared in 1839 there were areas of meadow land around the centre and at Lent Green; elsewhere arable farming was the norm, except where there were drainage problems and in the northern wooded areas. Some farmers, such as William Bayley junior, cultivated extensive tracts of large fields but, by contrast, in Lent Rise the fields were mainly small strips, mostly farmed by each owner's family. Here were long-established local people such as Winter, Winch, Britnell, Chadwick, Binfield, and Bayley. But Ann Aldridge farmed 800 acres and employed 50 labourers in East Burnham in 1851, and William Bayley junior farmed 640 acres around Britwell Farm with 20 labourers. Bayley's family had farmed in the Burnham area for five or six generations; in 1839 his father owned the brickfields where Lent Rise School now stands.

Other farmers included few locals, with the exception of Elisha Stannett at Dorneywood and James Austin of Horse Harness, whose colleague Giles Tombs came from Cowley in Gloucestershire; John Cross, George Crocker, Richard Cleare, Joseph Blinko, and William Webster came from as near as Hedgerley or from as far as Berkshire or Bedfordshire. The gentry and most landowners were not descended from local families. The list of the gentry, traders, publicans, railway servants or professional classes throughout the last two hundred years shows how mobile were the skilled and educated elements of the population, and how the wealth of the village was largely in the hands of 'outsiders'.

On the Dropmore estate Lady Grenville exercised a major influence after her husband's death in 1834. This was two years after the Reform Act removed the electoral advantage he hoped to gain by acquiring so much land and property, despite the difficulties of ensuring that tenants maintained it well. She died in 1864 with no issue and the estate passed to Lord Grenville's nephew, George Matthew Fortescue of Boconnoc in Cornwall, who became Lord of the Manor. His family gradually sold off the outer parts of the estate. In 1864 this included a large area in Hitcham bought

by George Hanbury, a brewer and hop merchant from London, who built a country house there called Blythewood, known later as Hitcham House. George Hanbury and his wife became contributors to many local causes, building the Reading Room and the School in Hitcham, and the Mission Hall in Burnham High Street. He was also founder of Paddington Green Children's Hospital and High Sheriff of Buckinghamshire in 1875.

After Lady Wells' death in 1842, Huntercombe Manor was let for Ascot Week, Henley Regatta, holidays and the like until 1871, when the Hon and Rev Richard Cavendish Boyle, younger brother of the eighth Earl of Cork and Orrery purchased it from the Fortescues. He and his wife after him lived there for 45 years. Mrs Boyle (the celebrated writer 'E.V.B.') created a fine garden visited by many eminent people, including her special friend the Empress Frederick, Queen Victoria's eldest daughter. She was a conscientious supporter of village activities, as Lady Grenville had been, including the Bible Classes and the Band of Hope. She made generous contributions to the restoration of St Peter's church and provided a funeral bier, which was dredged up from the village pond in recent years, still bearing her inscribed plaque. The road running past the west front of Huntercombe, from Burnham to Windsor, was diverted westwards in 1877 to prevent noisy carts disturbing E.V.B.'s beloved wildlife.

The Vicar was responsible for areas of land called Glebe, which in Burnham consisted of a few acres of meadow land between St Peter's church and Lent Green hamlet, used in 1839 mainly for livestock though, under another vicar, the drier areas might have been farmed.

South-east of the town lay the local water-mill, near the Two Mile Brook Inn (now the White Horse) where the Bath Road crossed the mill stream; variously named on maps as Hay, Aye, Eye etc Mill (reflecting the local accent), most people referred to it as Hillman's or Roger's Mill during the last hundred years. Grain was brought from all around, some farmers being obliged to use the mill as a condition of their farm tenancy.

When Samuel Christie-Miller died in 1889, his wife and only child having died in 1882 and 1884 respectively, Britwell Court passed to his nephew Wakefield Christy, who also took the surname Christie-Miller in 1890 and, between 1893 and 1896, added the south-east block and the main staircase. He diverted the original road along the front of the house, dividing it from the farms, and set it further north in its present position. The old road is still evident at the entrances to the estate on the Burnham and Britwell sides.

The property passed on Wakefield's death to his widow and then to his son Sydney Richardson in 1903. The family gave the west window and a lectern to the parish church, the land of which the Working Men's Club stands, and the lease of the land where the old village school stood. In 1919 the house and the main library were sold, the former to a religious community of nuns, the Servants of Christ, who added a chapel designed by the architect Sir Ninian Comper. They named the property the House of Prayer.

In 1903 Edward Clifton-Brown, a partner in the merchant banking firm of Brown, Shipley and Co, moved with his wife, formerly Dorothy Hanbury, to Burnham Grove, a large house north of Britwell Court. He purchased most of the land attached to Britwell Court, creating a 1,000 acre estate which included Britwell, Lynch Hill and Leas Farms, Cants Hill and Littlejohns Wood. He was noted for his Hampshire Down sheep and Berkshire and Tamworth pigs; in his year as High Sheriff he was nicknamed the 'High Shepherd of Bucks'.

During the last 150 years Burnham has expanded with increasing speed, the nature of farming has changed and housing developments and commercial premises now occupy what were once farmland or the gardens of large houses. Extraction of brickearth and gravel has left great hollows, which creates split-level gardens, and even roads such as Chiltern and Aldbourne Roads. A casual look at the dates of houses in Gore Road and Lent Rise Road shows how, from about 1880, expansion accelerated, with a mixture of speculative building for letting or sale and larger properties such as Fairfield, Sunny Croft and Bredward being built for more prosperous villagers, and for outsiders attracted by the location and the rail route to London.

Bredward, where the Close of that name has since been built, was bought in 1897 by W.H. Williams, Chief Surveyor and Estate Agent of the Great Western Railway, who wrote one of the ealier histories of Burnham, and was churchwarden of St Peter's for many years until his death in 1931. His wife started the first infant welfare clinic here during the Great War.

Further north, Lord Courtauld Thompson settled at Dorneywood in 1920 and enlarged this erstwhile farmhouse belonging to the Dorney Court estate. Filled with antique furniture, the late Rex Whistler's engagement to carry out a 'trompe l'oeil' scheme of decoration completed the transformation. The Thompson family is also commemorated in a family window in Dropmore church. On his death, the house, contents and land were left to the Dorneywood Trust, the house being for the use of a Minister of the Crown on the nomination of the Prime Minister. An outlying part of the estate has been leased to the local Scout Association and is used by Scouts and Guides from a wide area. Dropmore House and some surrounding land remained with the Fortescues until it was sold to Lord Kemsley just before the outbreak of the second world war.

Today, Burnham's former brick kilns are derelict, the related skills lost and lanes leading to them disused. Fields cover the site of Shaggs Lane, and Russells Cellar Lane (closed by Lord Grenville in 1812); Nearway Road is now merely a name on the title deeds of houses in East Field Road. Orchard Avenue, Bayley Crescent and Orchardgrove (the name of an erstwhile telephone exchange) evoke memories of fruit growing.

West Town Farm, dating back to the 'dark ages', has survived in Green Belt isolation as an effective symbol of Burnham's ever changing farming heritage, and nearby pre-Reformation Burnham Abbey has once again become an Abbey after 400 years as a farm.

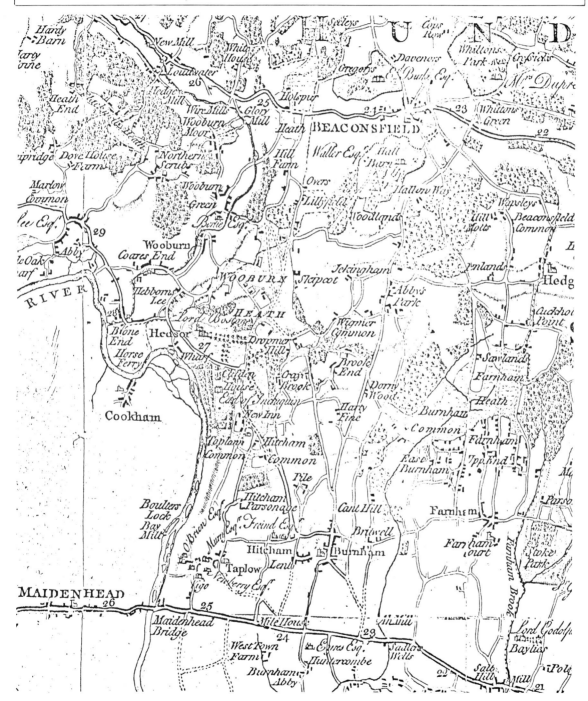

Part of the map of Buckinghamshire, by Thomas Jeffreys, 1788.
(CUL)

ADDRESS
FROM
THE MAGISTRATES
TO THE
Inhabitants of Burnham Division.

FELLOW COUNTRYMEN,

You have heard that there are persons going about the country setting fire to ricks and other property. It is our duty to call upon you to combine with us to discover the perpetrators. We call on ALL to come forward on such an occasion, but we particularly call on the

Honest and Industrious Labourers,

for on them the mischief arising from this destructive system will most severely fall. Destroying Corn must raise the price of Bread. Injuring the property of Farmers, and others, must lessen the means of employing labourers. Machinery for Manufactures makes Cheap Goods; breaking it, in the present state of trade, will give the Market to Foreigners, and stop work. Cases of real distress will be attended to if properly made known. Rioting will only increase distress. Do not then hesitate what part to take. Be faithful to your employers.—Be faithful to yourselves.—Give every assistance, every information you can to Magistrates, whose duty and whose anxious wish it is to protect and benefit you.—They, on their parts will use the most active exertions to preserve the peace and prosperity of the Country.

November 30, 1830.

[G. W. Wetton, Printer, Maidenhead.

LEFT: Notice displayed in 1830, during the uprising of agricultural workers; (BC/CRO) ABOVE: William Wyndham, Lord Grenville of Dropmore House, Prime Minister 1806-7; CENTRE: Eleanor Vere Boyle, and BELOW: Hicknham Farm. (BS)

ABOVE: Burnham Abbey Farm in the 19th century, showing the present chapel, centre; CENTRE: Lower Britwell Farm, and BELOW: Upper Britwell Farm.

33

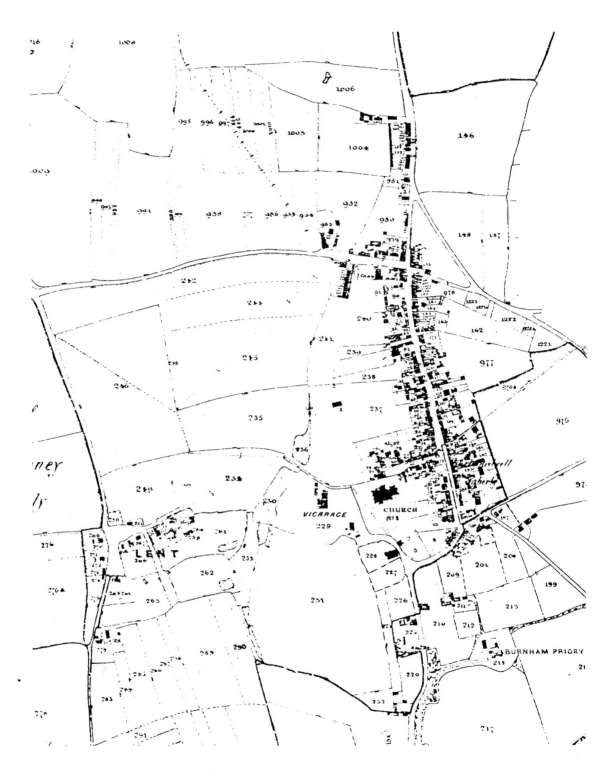

*Land ownership in Lent Field and nearby, based on the Tithe
Schedule and map, 1839. (ME/RI)*

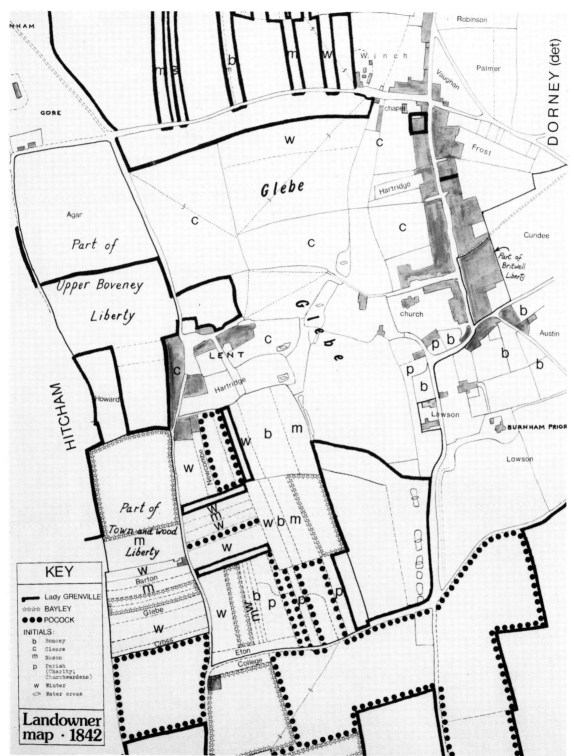

Land ownership in Lent Field and nearby, based on the Tithe
Schedule and Map, 1839. (ME/RI)

ABOVE LEFT: 'Tiggy' Bayley of the ancient farming family grew oranges and lemons at Lent Rise in 1940; (DD) RIGHT: Daniel Pusey, fruit farmer of Lent Green, with his family c1897; (DD) BELOW LEFT: Daniel Pusey's mother Elizabeth, born 1830, with her grandchildren c1900. (DD) CENTRE: Agricultural workers on the land now occupied by the Priory Estate, 1930, and BELOW: Starveall Farm, north of the Beeches. (BS)

ABOVE: Fred Cleare centre, with his threshing machine at Poyle Farm c1925; (MEC) CENTRE: Poyle Farmhouse as it is today, the old building having been refaced, and BELOW: the rear view of Haymill, from a painting by J. Herbert Snell, c1895. (BS)

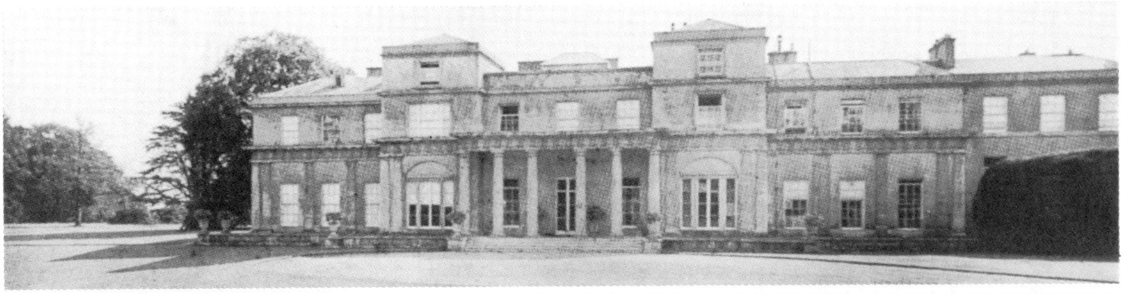
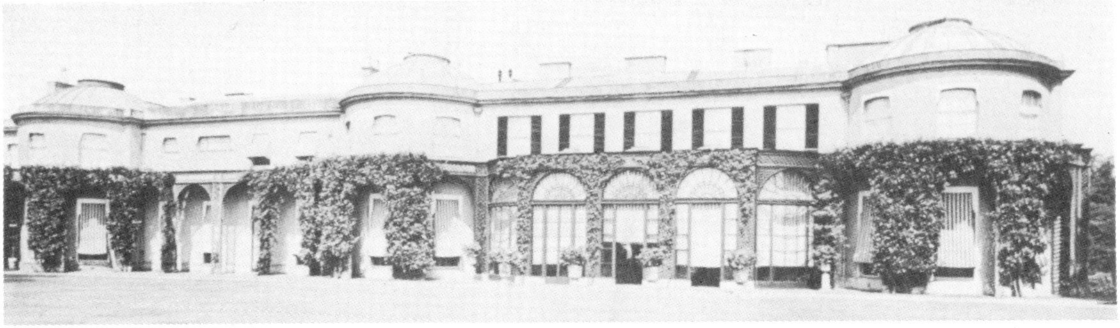
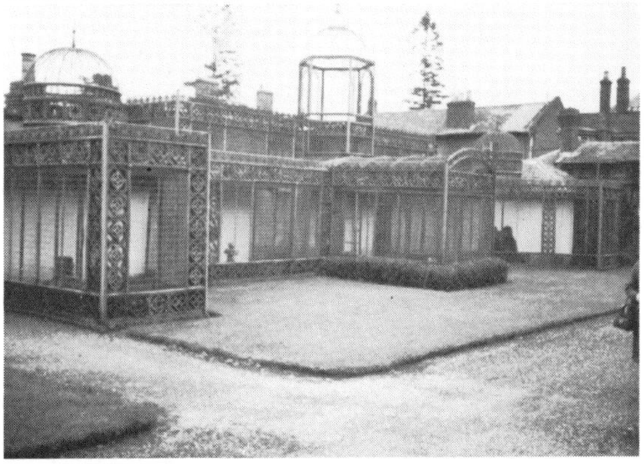
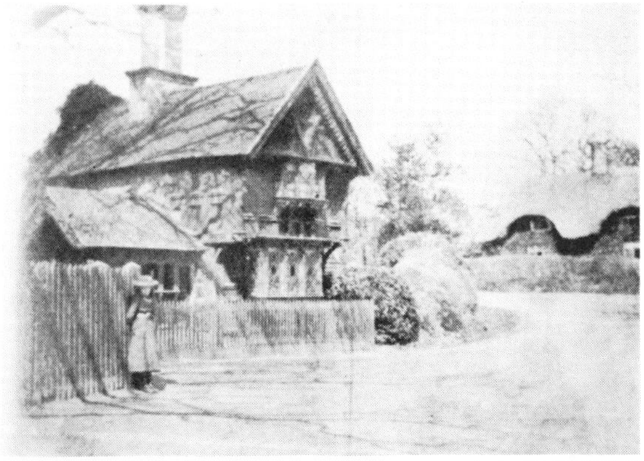
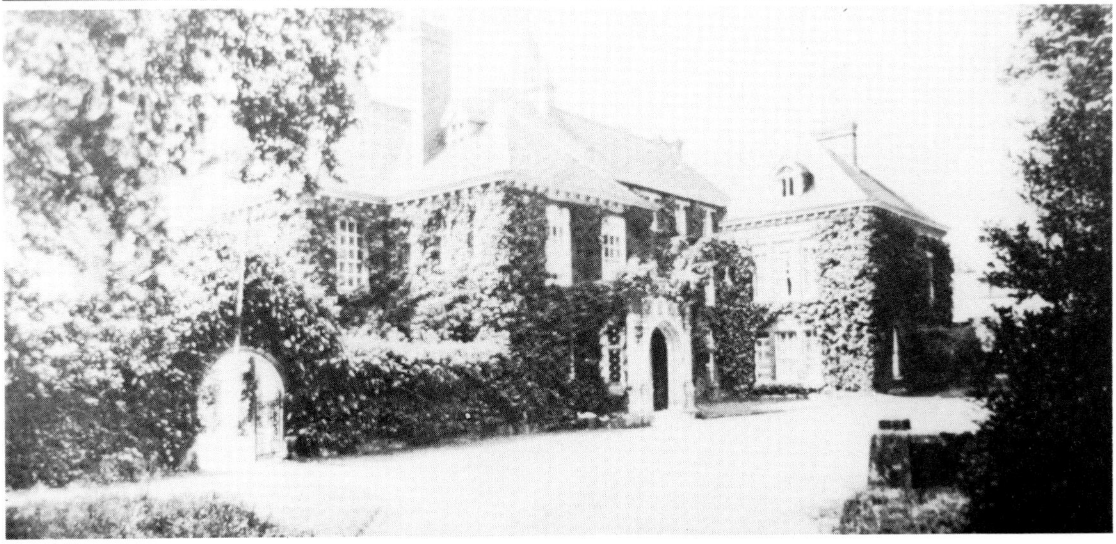

OPPOSITE ABOVE: Front entrance of Dropmore House, 1938, (BS) and CENTRE: garden entrance. (BS) LEFT: The Aviqry, Dropmore House, 1938, (BS) and RIGHT: NE Lodge, Dropmore Estate, which Lady Grenville had faced with carved panels from cabinets, and the village school right, 1905. (EM) BELOW: Britwell Court, main entrance in the 16th century part of of the building, 1919. (RM) ABOVE: East face of Britwell Court, 1919, showing the conservatory, centre, to which the chapel was later joined, (RM) and BELOW: hall and main stairway, added to Britwell Court in the 19th century. (RM)

39

ABOVE: Slough Lodge, the south entrance to Britwell Court Estate, in Lower Britwell Road, 1919, (RM) and BELOW: S.R. Christie-Miller's study in Britwell Court, 1919. (RM)

ABOVE: The library, Britwell Court, built by S. Christie-Miller, to house his famous collection, (1919); LEFT: now a private entrance to Britwell Court Estate, this was originally the main road, diverted to its present position north of Upper Britwell Farm, seen here on the left, and RIGHT: south face of Huntercombe Manor House, as it was in E.V. Boyle's time, 1871-1915. (EM)

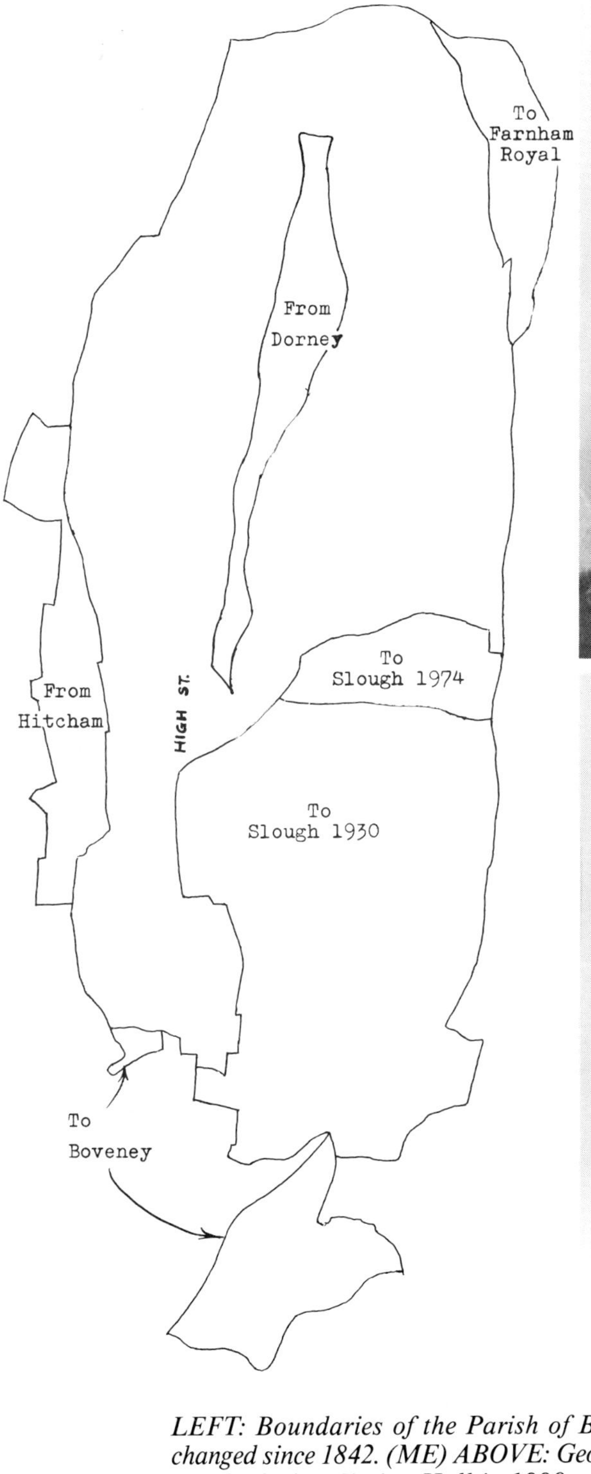
To
Farnham
Royal
From
Dorney
To
Slough 1974
From
Hitcham
HIGH ST.
To
Slough 1930
To
Boveney

LEFT: Boundaries of the Parish of Burnham and how they have changed since 1842. (ME) ABOVE: George Hanbury of 'Blythewood', who built the Mission Hall in 1880, and BELOW: his wife Mary. (FP)

ABOVE LEFT: The east face of Huntercombe Manor House, as it is today; RIGHT: the Burnham Priory, built c1824. As a private residence c1920. (BS) CENTRE: The Grove, (now a hotel) as the residence of E. Clifton-Brown c1903. Formerly called Cant's Hill, it was owned by an uncle of Thomas Gray, who stayed there; (FP) BELOW LEFT: Edward Clifton-Brown married Dolly Hanbury 1897, (FP) and RIGHT: Mr & Mrs E. Clifton-Brown 1940. (FP)

ABOVE LEFT: Children of Edward and Dolly Clifton-Brown, Rhona, Geoffrey and Anthony, (FP) and BELOW: wearing a trilby hat, E. Clifton-Brown with one of his famous flock of South-Down sheep. (FP) ABOVE RIGHT: William H. Williams 1892, historian and churchwarden for many years, (KL) and BELOW: Mrs W.H. Williams 1909, who started an Infant Welfare Clinic in 1914. (KL)

LEFT: 'Bredward', W.H. Williams' house 1900. An estate bearing the same name now covers the site; (KL) RIGHT: Dorney Wood House, (BS) and BELOW: Hawthorn Lane, Burnham Common, c1910. Most of the woodland north of here is now part of Burnham Beeches.

BURNHAM.

CATALOGUE OF THE

HOUSEHOLD FURNITURE

AND EFFECTS,

Which will be Sold by Auction by

MESSRS.

BUCKLAND & SONS

(Instructed by Mr. Cleare),

At THE FARM, HIGH STREET, BURNHAM,

(lately in the occupation of Miss Cleare),

On Thursday, December 21st, 1905

At ONE o'clock precisely,

COMPRISING

Walnut and Mahogany Chests of Drawers,

Marble-top Washstands and Fittings, Swing Toilet Glasses, French and other Bedsteads and Bedding, Fenders and Fireirons,

Drawing Room Suite in Saddlebags,

Whatnots, Oak and Beach Chairs, Circular-top and Pembroke Tables, Mantel Glasse, Hall Stand, Kitchen Utensils, Crockery, &c.

3 Sets of Double Harness & 3 Riding Saddles

and other Effects.

On View Morning of Sale.   Catalouges may be obtained of

Messrs. BUCKLAND & SONS, Auctioneers,

4, Bloomsbury Square, London,
118, High Street, Slough, and Windsor.

T. E. LUFF, PRINTER, ST. LEONARD'S ROAD, AND THAMES STREET.

Notice of sale of effects from Cleare's farm house, Burnham High Street, 1905. (BC/CRO)

FAITH AND CHARITY

Dominated by the Parish Church, the 19th century 'town' of Burnham was a smaller and more compact community than it is today. Mostly of 13th and 14th century construction, St Peter's is the oldest building in Burnham, and was much altered over the years; in 1800 a stunted wooden construction capped its tower.

The Vestry was the governing body exercising both civil and ecclesiastical authority, consisting of the Vicar and two Churchwardens as principal officers, and others drawn mainly from ratepayers such as tenant farmers, shopkeepers, traders and the like. Funds to maintain local amenities derived from parish rates, glebe rents, local subscribers and legacies left by benefactors, while two Overseers elected annually kept the accounts, and the Poor Rate, levied on property owners, catered for the needs of the unemployed.

Between 1553 and 1831, bequests from 18 benefactors led to charities for specific purposes, eg in 1722 Elizabeth Robinson left £20 a year to educate three boys and three girls, while Henry Sayer in 1810 left £20 a year for bread for the poor at Christmas. Churchwardens were personally responsible for distributing food etc to the most needy in the parish.

The Workhouse was built in 1763. When drafting the rules, Vicar Stephen Apthorne decreed that children in the Workhouse must learn to read, yet the first National School was not built until three vicars and 50 years later. Standing on glebe land, the Workhouse was south of the Church, where St Peter's Close is now, housing paupers of Burnham Parish only, whereas the National School, built on the Gore in 1811, was to serve Burnham, Hitcham and Taplow. The school was governed by the Church authority, which considered it part of the Vicar's religious duty to educate the poor. Each day began with the Vicar or curate taking the catechism, to ensure the children learned to be reverent, as well as to read and write.

Vestry minutes of 1798 record that 37 families living out of the Workhouse were paid sums, revised monthly, from 1s to 6s 8d a week. Other expenses were £21 salary for John Greer, the master, £7 6s 9d for three militia men, 1s to a soldier with a pass, 14s to William Lane for a pig, 6s 6d to Mr Larking for a hog trough and 11s to William Webb to make a drain round the Workhouse.

When demands were made that year, for 137 men from the parish for draft into the Old Militia, 94 people paid 3s into the Parish Club, to provide substitutes. These included six farmers, 19 servants, 31 labourers, two bakers, three butchers, three gardeners, two carpenters, seven shoemakers, a hostler, shepherd, coachman and others. Obviously all were liable for conscription and those unable to afford 3s became unwilling participants in the Napoleonic Wars.

In 1788, the Workhouse had 45 occupants. By 1821, numbers had dwindled to 24 while, in 1828, only 18 persons remained, whose combined ages amounted to 1,113 years. Paupers in Burnham were well cared for, since the master's account in 1790 shows Mr Honey, butcher, was paid 6d per head per week, and Messrs Austin,

Webster and Winter were collectively paid 1s 10d per head per week for other goods. Later on, the Vestry invited tenders to clothe the Workhouse inmates. In 1815, John Boulter won the contract at 4s 6d per head per week. By 1819, not surprisingly, competition became more intense, and three other contenders put in bids from 4s 2d to 5s, so John Boulter dropped his terms to 4s, winning the contract again. When shoes cost 3s 4d a pair and breeches 4s 3d, this was a lucrative game.

Registered apprenticeships in Burnham in the 1820s included Hester Johnson aged 17, apprenticed as a housewife for 4 yrs to John Rodgers of Hereford at a fee of £20, James Binfield 16, as a shoemaker to John Holman of Boveney for 5 years at £4 and William Pool 17, as a shoemaker to Lot Pulbrook of Burnham, for 4 years at £12. These were large sums for poor parents to find and were probably paid by the Overseers.

Bad weather caused high unemployment among agricultural labourers in 1817, so the Vestry organised work for them. Payment for a 10 hour day, for boys 10-13 years was 5d, for boys 13-16 years 7d; a married man with no children got 1s, while a married man with four children received 2s. However, no relief was given to those owning a dog or gun, perhaps a disincentive to potential poachers.

A workhouse punishment was a spell in the stocks, on the south side of Church Street, near the present fire station. Another was 'time in the Penitentiary', or 'cage'. In 1839 concern was shown over its lack of security, so two strong locks were fitted. Three years later, there was still anxiety about keeping prisoners confined, so Mr Webb altered the positions of the cage and engine house doors, yet it was not until 1854 that a new 'Lock up House' was built on the site of the old engine house and cage, at that time called the Parade, on the South East corner of Church Street. The Pound for stray animals was in Hogfair Lane.

The Vestry may have ruled the parishioners' lives, but not all their souls, for non-conformity had returned to Burnham in the late 1700s, after many years' absence. John Cooke, Independent Minister of Maidenhead, would walk thence to meetings in a house in Church Street. A great deal of verbal and active opposition was meted out to him and his followers, but determination and faith won in the end. A site was offered by Mr Coleshill, financial backing by brewer John Langton, and the building of Zion Chapel came about in 1791. In Gore Road, the Chapel is now used as a warehouse but, while worship continued there, the road between Almond Road and the High Street was called Chapel Street. Rev George Newbury became the first full-time minister in 1824, when membership was 24. Most members were local tradesmen, including Winch, Simmons, Dornell, Tilbury, Crocker, Hyde and Baldwin, and some of them supported Anglican activities as well.

A need for more school rooms induced the Vestry to accept an offer by Thomas Carter, Vicar, in 1843, to build an infant school on the site of the Workhouse. The Union District Workhouse, built in Slough in 1831, would have taken the occupants from Burnham, so the building was no longer in use.

When extra burial ground was needed at St Peter's, a piece between the vicarage garden wall and the south gate of the churchyard was taken over. It cost £10 2s for the Bishop to consecrate it in 1834.

Poor Law Commissioners upset the locals by accusing Mr Williams of appropriating funds, and dismissed him as Relieving Officer in 1841. To show respect for his 30 years' faithful service, local folk gave him an inscribed silver salver.

George Newbury retired as Independent Minister in 1843, on a pension of £15. He died in 1849 and his tombstone remains propped against the old chapel wall, having been removed from the Burial Ground when a church hall was built upon it. A family grave at the Chapel cost 1 gn for members, 2 gns for strangers, plus 5s per burial. Mr Popley became the next minister, though his stay was short, followed by James Edmunds, who replied when accepting the post in 1848: 'We are the Dissenters from the Church of England for conscience sake, - - - - we no longer suffer from cruel and oppressive laws, afflicting our persons, abridging our religious liberties, or goading us to forsake the land of our forefathers, to seek asylum in a foreign clime, - - - - the prayers and self denying patriotism of the 17th century have prevailed - - - -. Let us then cultivate a catholic spirit towards all genuine Christians of every denomination - - - - in so doing, we shall best sustain the honour of Dissent - - - -.' James Edmunds started 'circulating' prayer meetings and continued to use the 'Regester' started by George Newbury. One of the last entries notes that 1 cwt of lead sheet was stolen from the Chapel porch.

Suspicion reared its head in the parish in 1850, as a report says: 'The somnambulant state of Burnham, has been started from its quietude by a "beating of arms", in the form of handbills advertising a public meeting - - - - to investigate Charities belonging to the parish'. The meeting lacked support, but Vicar Carter and Churchwardens Bayley and Webster felt obliged to reassure the complainants that the charities were fairly distributed.

In lighter vein, the church choir gave a concert in the Infant School in 1862, to raise Glee Club funds and celebrate the retirement of Miss Clayton as organist. Benjamin Baldwin was chief organiser, while Messrs Almond, Hebbes and Roberts rendered solo items to a packed audience.

Wesleyan-Methodists held spasmodic meetings in the 1830s, but it was 1862-3 before they were established here. A Burnham Mission Committee was set up, followed later by two Society Stewards, appointed to meet local needs. One of these, Brother Lake, stepped out of line in 1869, by preaching at Slough, instead of Burnham. Charles Cleare, the butcher's son, was converted from an Anglican upbringing to Methodism. He later became post-master in Maidenhead, after marrying Elizabeth, a grand-daughter of John Furness, one of John Wesley's ministers, though he preached away from Burnham, perhaps due to his father's opposition to his conversion.

No improvements were made to the Parish Church while John Roberts and George Bethell were Vicars and, by 1863, major restoration was necessary. At that time 276 seats were available, only 20 of which were free. Thomas Carter was 89, when he and Churchwarden Samuel Christie-Miller, of Britwell Court, raised £2,000 by subscription. The gallery was removed and oak pews installed to seat 400 or more, all free. Among other things, heating was put in and five buttresses added to

fortify the outside walls. Thomas Carter was a much loved Vicar, whose prowess is clear, since 100 confirmations took place in 1862. He was succeeded by his son William Adolphus, six years later.

By then, organisations initiated by the church sprang up like mushrooms. The Women's Clothing Club, Penny Bank Children's Club, Girls' and Young Mens' Friendly Societies met fortnightly, and all local notables contributed to the Society for the Propogation of the Gospel.

Robert Rumsey, who became Vicar in 1878, was a considerable live wire. He started night school for lads, played in the village cricket team, invested in surplices for the choir, (which impressed the Bishop), and instigated lavish decorations in church at Christmas. Excessive beer drinking was disliked by the Temperance Society, who made some efforts in 1883 to reduce it. A Coffee Tavern opened in the High Street while the curate, Rev Banting, organised a Harvest Savings Club. Harvesters were encouraged to pay their wages into the Club, instead of spending them on beer. An incentive was given, ie a bonus to be paid with a lump sum at the end. As harvesting is thirsty work, a suggestion for a refreshing drink during working hours was — ½ lb oatmeal, ½ lb sugar, ¼ lb cocoa mixed with a gallon of water.

George Hanbury paid for the Mission Hall, built in 1880. Now a greengrocer's shop, it stands opposite the entrance to Church Street, originally designed as a place for worship and recreation. Harry Williams, a lay preacher, affectionately called 'Bogey', ran it under the auspices of the Parish Church. Services there were designed for the working man, who felt the Church was too highbrow, and there was no obligation to put money in the collection.

The Church choir sang carols on Christmas Day at 4.0 pm in those days, a custom many might wish to see revived, while the Hand Bell Ringers offered to practise in people's homes free of charge. A Drum and Fife Band for lads was started in 1888, which proved to be popular for several years. It was organised by the Temperance Society with Robert Rumsey as president, George Garnett, corporal and Fred Addaway, lance corporal.

By 1884, yet more burial ground was needed. A piece of land next to the school in Church Street was purchased from Mr Cleare for £200, and consecrated in 1885. The Vicar had great difficulty persuading parishioners they could no longer be buried in the old churchyard; how history repeats itself.

Vicar Rumsey was in some ways a controversial figure. On one occasion, giving less than the required devotion at a funeral, he was obliged to apologise to the deceased's family. On another, George Hanbury accused him of popish rituals, but this time he maintained he was given the right to absolve sins and the Lincoln judgment upheld this view. He was generally held in high esteem, involving himself in many spheres of parish life, including advising the unemployed on emigration and becoming a Diocesan School Inspector.

Samuel Christie-Miller, Churchwarden and devoted benefactor for 20 years, died in 1889. His wish to have the Church Tower restored was realised two years later, when the Norman windows were discovered, the belfy turret built, a sixth bell added and the present elegant spire built onto the tower. Chief subscribers were Wakefield

Christie-Miller, Robert Rumsey, George Hanbury, Captain Farwell, Mr Dickinson and Mrs E.V. Boyle. Two more bells were added a few years later, making a total of eight.

Thenceforth, the Vestry were concerned with ecclesiastical matters only, as the Parish Council, set up in 1894, dealt with civic affairs.

By the 1890s, Methodism had' come to stay. A decision to form a Lent Rise Leaders' Meeting meant severing the former connection with Maidenhead. Burnham Brick Co owner, George Wethered offered land for sale at Lent Rise, on the corner of Nearway Road, now Eastfield so, in 1896, the Wesleyan Chapel was built there. Low membership meant a financial struggle yet, by 1906, with a membership of 67, a Sunday School room was built and free seats were available to those unable to pay rents for pews.

The annual custom of 'Beating the Bounds' of the Parish was still observed. It took place at Rogation Tide, starting with an 8 am service; then the Vicar, curate, choir and other interested parties, started on the round. Vans with food and drink were stationed at convenient spots, while choir boys were 'bumped' at various points, so that all would be sure where the boundary lay.

A silver tea and coffee service was presented to Robert and Mrs Rumsey, on the occasion of their silver wedding anniversary. Two years later, in 1900, Robert resigned after 20 years as Vicar. Said to be in need of a less taxing parish, he exchanged livings with George Willes of Calverton, the great-grandson of Mr Justice Willes, Solicitor General in 1766, whose memorial is in St Peter's Church. George Willes was a sick man when he came to Burnham, and within months had died, but he was given an impressive funeral.

Frederick Fitzpatrick Penruddock was next to grace St Peter's pulpit. In his first year, a new curate, Mr Cartright, and organist Mr Swaffield were appointed, and a Flower Service introduced. All was not sweetness and light however, for a certain gentleman, chosen by Mr Swaffield to sing the anthem at Harvest Festival, caused the choir to absent themselves or refuse to sing, to demonstrate their strong objection.

For almost 100 years the Grenvilles and later, the Fortescues of Dropmore, used the north transept in St Peter's as a family pew, with a private entrance. The carved oak panelling there, depicting religious scenes, was purchased by A.M. Fortescue, on the continent. In 1902, they absolved themselves from further right to it, and the responsibility for its upkeep, but donated £100 to the restoration fund.

The same year, George Dalgleish retired as pastor at Zion Chapel, now called the Congregational Church. He created a precedent during his 11 years there, by being photographed with fellow brethren, apparently the only pastor to do so for many decades. At the Mission Hall that year, the Harvest Home was held on a Thursday, so the Vicar and curate could attend. Mr Hanbury gave the address and a special collection for the Windsor Infirmary, 'The Poor Mens Home for Sickness', raised £6, a large sum from poor people.

Vicar Penruddock suspected children when a break-in occurred at the Church. The intruders had rifled the poor box and regaled themselves with the communion

wine. As a keen chorister, he had good reason to be proud of the choir in 1910. It boasted 16 men and 13 boys. Oliver Watts was head boy and 'Chunky' Knight, landlord of the Feathers, was among the senior contingent. Urged by the Vestry to charge fees for erecting crosses in the churchyard, the Vicar resisted the idea, though he did prohibit artificial flowers on graves. He retired in 1913, by which time the Burnham Consolidated Charities were set up, to rationalise incomes from small bequests. Thomas Buchanan Carter, who succeeded him, stayed only three years and was obliged by the Parish Council to number and record graves during his term. His successor, Percy Pleydell Nott, was a disciplinarian who put the fear of God into many youngsters, although the parish took him to their hearts. During his early years here, responsibility for looking after the Parish Church, churchyard and Church of England Schools was taken over by the Parochial Church Council, set up in 1919.

By then the war had taken its toll of Burnham families, whose dead were venerated at the consecration and unveiling of the War Memorial, on 19 December 1920. Erected then between the Infant School and Workmen's Institute, it was moved to its present site in 1965. Eighty seven names were inscribed there, including Walter Lewington, who returned in 1921, after six years' absence, to find himself a posthumous hero.

By 1932, the many branches of the Wesleyan-Methodist movement were brought together under one umbrella, with the result that the building at Lent Rise then became the Methodist Church. It continued to thrive, attracting members from all walks of life, running cultural as well as religious activities. By 1957 new buildings, including a vestry and large hall, were erected for over £9,000. Inspired by minister Rev Raymond Lenten, forty Church members worked hard to raise £1,600 towards the cost. Local post master Frederick Moon and his wife Elsie were outstanding workers for the Church.

Roman Catholics were celebrating mass in the 1920s, first in the Council Rooms, over the fire station, then in the house in Britwell Road called 'Fairfield'. The first Roman Catholic church was built in 1935 in Lower Britwell Road. A wooden construction, it took three weeks to build, costing £500, paid for by subscription at 2s 6d per head per week. Father Brennan became the first full time priest in 1940. Irish immigrants who had settled at Cippenham, followed by Italian prisoners of war who chose to remain here, swelled the local Roman Catholic population considerably. By the time Noel Burditt became priest in 1948, the church had been enlarged and a social hall built next to it.

In 1959 the original Church was demolished, and the site given to a community of nuns, the Sisters of St Mary of Namur. A new Church, Our Lady of Peace, which had been built next to the earlier one, was blessed and opened in 1958. The foundations were dug, and 180 tonnes of concrete mixed, by men of the parish, under the architect's supervision, before the contractors took over. Father Burditt, who remained until the early 1960s, was succeeded by Father Woodward.

In the meantime, Herbert Hulm had become Parish Clerk and Verger at St Peter's in 1923, a post he held for 46 years. He soon became indispensible to Percy Nott and successive Vicars, taking much of their work on himself to relieve their load. Herbert had a special aura about him, and his booming 'amens' still echo through the church. His patience was sorely tried on one occasion, when the undertaker arrived with a funeral party of which he knew nothing. The Vicar played the organ to the mourners for two hours, while Herbert broke all records digging the grave. Harold Rhodes, affectionately known as 'Sally', was organist and choirmaster for many years and travelled everywhere on a huge green bicycle. He and later Lloyd Willimot encouraged talented choirboys to train for entrance to Eton College Choir School. Herbert Hulm's son Robert, David Derrick and Malcolm Tegg were among the many who succeeded. In the 1940s, Bill Walker as head boy got 1d per practice, 2d per service and 6d for weddings and funerals.

George Gilbert, bell ringer extraordinary, came to Burnham in 1932 and revolutionised the Bell Tower. Where formerly ringers were paid, George formed a voluntary band, 'St Peter's Society of Change Ringers', recruiting choirboys of 9-12 years and training them to become competent ringers. Within two years they rang a peal of 500 changes, taking three hours non-stop to complete it. With an average age of 14½ years, the band was the youngest to perform such a feat. The Society, captained by Gordon Limmer, was recognised as one of the most enthusiastic in the country.

Percy Nott resigned in 1937, after 21 years as Vicar. The next year, Edward Clifton-Brown paid for the Coronation Service of George VI to be broadcast in the Church, the highlight of Hugh Read's first year as Vicar.

Within a matter of months, the second world war began. The bellringers were of conscription age, leaving George Gilbert with no band and a ban on bellringing for the duration. Not to be thwarted, he trained a group of 9-12 year old girls, using silent bells. When hostilities had ceased, Burnham had given up another 48 men, four of whom were bellringers, but George and his band achieved a Victory Peal.

James Wildman became Vicar in 1943, having served as Chaplain in the Merchant Navy. Like many of his predecessors, he lived in the old vicarage next to St Peter's. Having been almost rebuilt in 1838, it was a rambling house, with no conveniences and 28 rooms, mostly riddled with dry rot. James struggled to maintain it, but he was to be the final resident of this elegant building. His early years at Burnham endeared him to his parishioners. With the aid of Charles Griffiths, Churchwarden and former headmaster of the school, he started a Church Youth Club, giving so many of us a social focus after the war.

As the 1940s advanced, George Gilbert was determined to improve the sound of his beloved bells. His enthusiasm inspired the whole village and, after organising 'Bells Parades' etc, his trojan effort was rewarded in 1949, when seven of the eight bells were recast at a cost of £2,000. To the new tenor bell were added the names: James Wildman — Vicar, A.H. Packe and Dr M.H. Summers — Churchwardens, and George Gilbert — ring master.

SUMMONED BY BELLS

LEFT: Congregational Church group c1898. Front row: Emily Butler aged 5, Rev Dalgleish, his wife and Ann Cleare; (MEC) RIGHT: George Gilbert's Band, trained on muffled bells, who rang the Victory Peal in 1945. Mary Jaycock, Hilda Taylor, Joyce Hearn, Jean Broomfield, Gwen Murkett, Freda Murkett, Mary Pemberton; (MJ) BELOW: with an average age of 14½ years, St Peter's bellringers were the youngest in the country to ring a peal of 500 changes in 1934: Pat Cashman, Ron Taylor, John Taylor, Jim Taylor, Bill Cyster, Norman Bristow. (JT)

*LEFT: George Gilbert, Ringmaster at St Peter's 1932-1960; (SPB)
CENTRE: casting St Peter's new tenor bell in 1949, are Taylor's of
Loughborough; (SPB) RIGHT: Rev Thomas Carter, vicar 1833-
1868; BELOW: south face of St Peter's from 1864-1891. (BS)*

LEFT: Local craftsman Mr Chown made the wrought iron work for the door to the base of the Tower of St Peter's. ABOVE CENTRE: Rev William Carter, vicar 1868-1878; RIGHT: Rev Robert Rumsey, vicar 1878-1901; CENTRE: Rev George Willes, vicar 1901; RIGHT: Rev Frederick Penruddock, vicar 1901-1914; BELOW: left to right: Rev Thomas B. Carter, vicar 1914-1916, Rev Percy Nott, vicar 1916-1937, Rev Hugh Read, vicar 1937-1943, and Rev James Wildman, vicar 1943-1977.

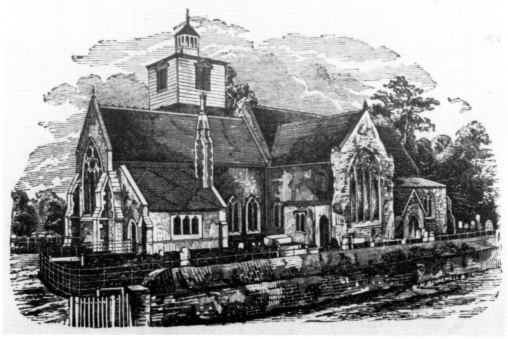

ABOVE: North face of St Peter's prior to the 1863 restoration, (BS)
and BELOW: after restoration. (WM)

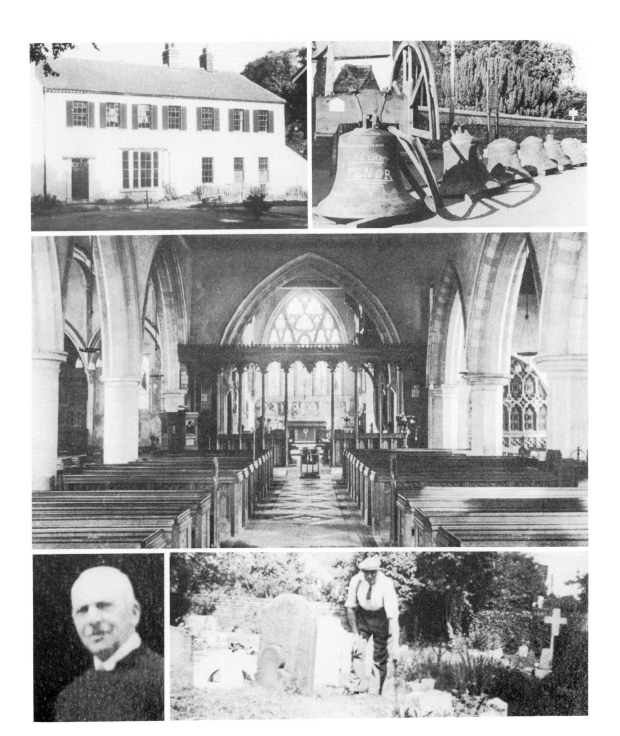

ABOVE LEFT: The old Rectory prior to demolition c1965. (LR) RIGHT: seven of the eight bells removed from St Peter's belfry, prior to recasting in 1949; (BS) CENTRE: interior of St Peter's, the differently faced pillars clearly visible.   BELOW LEFT: Herbert Hulm, parish clerk and verger of St Peter's, 1923-1969, (BS) and RIGHT: Herbert Hulm, in his 'Garden of Eden'. (BS)

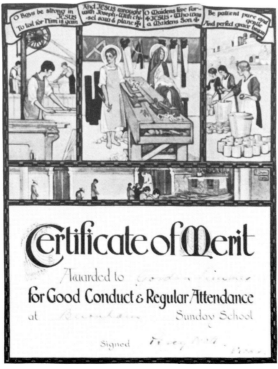

LEFT: *A monument to the Eyre family in St Peter's, brasses dating from the 16th century; ABOVE: and another to the Eyre family dated 1650. BELOW: Typical Sunday School certificate, signed by Rev Percy Nott 1925. (GL)*

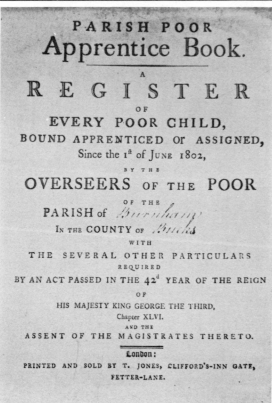

ABOVE: St Peter's choir 1908. Standing: C. Blackman, Bristow, ?, Taylor, G. Coombs, Welsh, Dobson, ?, ?, B. Walker, F. Lloyd, R. Lloyd. Centre: Painter, Jones, Walker, Starkey, Rev Penruddock, Rhodes, Winch, Knight, Taylor. Front: ?, Potter, Walker, Taylor, O. Watts, Neighbour, Walker, ?, Taylor. (OW) LEFT: Cover of the Burnham Parish Apprentice book 1802, (BC/CRO) and RIGHT: the War Memorial 1920, when the rifle bayonet was still in its place. (BS)

ABOVE: Dedication service 1946, for those lost 1939-1945; the Infant School behind was demolished 1962. (BS) LEFT: Looking south from the War Memorial into Stomp Road, the Priory wall was still there c1950; (BS) RIGHT: Zion Chapel, Gore Road built 1791. It later became the Congregational Church, now a warehouse. (BS)

*ABOVE: Interior of Our Lady of Peace, Roman Catholic Church,
built in Lower Britwell Road, 1935; (FW) BELOW: St Peter's from
the south west, between 1871, when the school, left, was built, and
1891, when the spire was added to the church tower. (BS)*

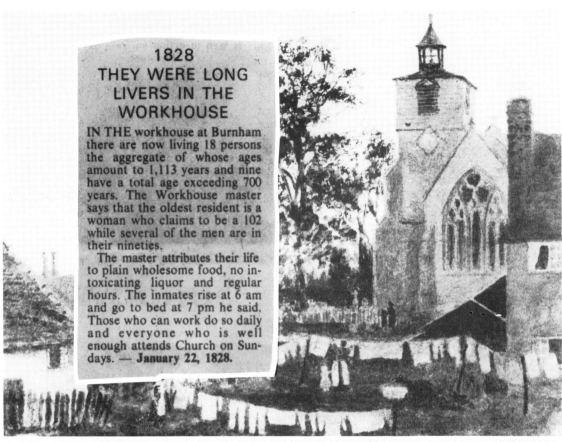

1828
THEY WERE LONG LIVERS IN THE WORKHOUSE

IN THE workhouse at Burnham there are now living 18 persons the aggregate of whose ages amount to 1,113 years and nine have a total age exceeding 700 years. The Workhouse master says that the oldest resident is a woman who claims to be a 102 while several of the men are in their nineties.

The master attributes their life to plain wholesome food, no intoxicating liquor and regular hours. The inmates rise at 6 am and go to bed at 7 pm he said. Those who can work do so daily and everyone who is well enough attends Church on Sundays. — **January 22, 1828.**

ABOVE: From a painting of St Peter's — from the east. The chimneys (left) are about where the Workhouse stood until 1844; (BS) INSET: a report on the Burnham Workhouse 1928 (by courtesy of the Windsor Slough & Eton Express). BELOW: The Lent Rise Wesleyan Chapel, built in 1896, when Nearway Road (now Eastfield), reached only to the hedge in the distance. (BS)

Children outside the Mission Hall, built between the bakery and the
George Hotel, in the High Street 1880. (BS)

A BETTER WAY OF LIFE

After 1784 Mail coaches ran regularly along the Bath Road through Maidenhead, and from there letters arrived in Burnham by foot post every morning at 8 am and were dispatched at 5 pm. William Swabey was the post master and from him the gentry and traders collected their letters. The postman and the policeman were not yet an integral part of village life.

For hundreds of years the keeping of law and order had been the responsibility of the parish constables, who were elected annually together with the Overseers and Headboroughs and other local officials, who administered the parish. There was no police force in Buckinghamshire until 1856, and even then parish constables remained as civilian officials until the end of the century.

The magistrates met on the first and third Monday every month in the George, which was more comfortable than the room built for the purpose in Church Street. In 1851 charges brought before Rev Carter, Mr Irby and Mr Bird at Burnham Petty sessions included: James Burnham and John Cullam — shooting pheasant on Mr Gurden's land (fined £1 14s 6d, and two months imprisonment, respectively). Thomas Blackman, John Bovington, William and James Shelton and William Langley — damaging a live fence, (fined 13s 8d each) and a man from Farnham Royal — stealing 1½ pints of wheat chaff, value 1d, from his employer, (allowed bail of £20).

The Fire Engine House accommodated a wooden manual pump, pushed along by 'helpers'. Buckets of water were poured in at the top, and levers at the sides squirted water out of the hoses. The helpers who worked these were known as 'squirters'.

The idea of a Fire Brigade had first been mooted in the village in 1795, but sufficient money was not forthcoming until 1810, when Henry Sayer of Huntercombe Manor left £100 in his will to start a fund for an engine.

A year later, the incumbents of Burnham, Hitcham and Taplow were given permission to enclose ½ acre of the common land on Burnham Gore, to erect a school for the poor children of the three parishes, 'subject to an annual quit rent of sixpence to the Lord of the Manor every Michaelmas'. The school was supported by voluntary subscriptions, and several charities, including £500 left by Lady Ravensworth in 1796 'to provide education for twelve poor girls'. The school buildings still stand on the Gore as three pairs of cottages.

In a letter to the parish magazine of 1870, Nathaniel Filbey of Winsconsin USA wrote '. . . I have been absent from Burnham the home of my childhood since 1832 . . . I married a daughter of Mr Hawthorne, formerly a master of Burnham Gore School where I was educated. Several names of the inhabitants are still familiar to me . . . Baldwin, Cleare, Roberts, Cutler, Winch, Webb, Lett and Stratton . . .'.

This school served the village for sixty years, although an additional Infant School was built in 1844 to the south of Burnham Church. Schools were built in Hitcham and Taplow in 1869 and 1848, and in 1871 the Gore school closed and a new school for 140 children was built at the west end of Church Street.

By 1842, Burnham had two surgeons, Jerome Barret, and William Roberts, who was also responsible for attending the poor of Burnham and Stoke Poges. Charged by the Vicar of Stoke Poges with neglecting his patients there, he claimed that his salary was insufficient and asked for £45 a year for his duties, to include all fractures, operations, coroners' inquests, vaccinations, midwifery when extra assistance was required, and supplying trusses at 12s each. Some years later Mr Barnshaw of Burnham had a fall while working in the chalk pit. He broke his thigh, and was rushed to Windsor Infirmary where it was set by Mr Bullock the horse surgeon.

In 1876 a Workmen's Reading Room in Church Street replaced the one in the High Street. It had a lending library of 550 books and was supported by 'honorary subscriptions and payments of members'. James Elliott and Alfred Heald were secretary and librarian when it was enlarged in 1883 and the improved facilities were inaugurated with a dinner and concert.

When the Bucks Constabulary was formed in 1856 the most efficient and experienced parish constables were recruited to form the first police force. John Symington, superintendent of the parish constables of Burnham, was appointed Superintendent of Police for the Slough division of the county. A few years earlier John Symington had charged a man with driving a horse and cart without holding the reins — he was fined 1s 6d. In his capacity as Inspector of Weights and Measures, Symington fined John Hillman, Job Roberts, William Litts, William Oakes and John Snapes, all Burnham beer retailers, for serving unjust measures. John Hersey was also fined, though less, because his measures were too large.

Each police division had two inspectors, a sergeant and three constables. The constables were paid between 17s and 20s a week. They wore frock coats, and top hats strengthened inside with cane, which could be used for standing on to see over high walls, or the heads of crowds. They were armed with sticks, but allowed to carry a cutlass where it was necessary for their protection. Election days were the times when they had to deal with the most unruly crowds.

The Vestry continued to elect parish constables for civil duties. In 1862 Robert Farmer was superintendent of constables. At the Petty Sessions William Paget, Thomas Pithers and David Black were charged with stealing apples from Robert Pimmer, market gardener. Being old offenders, they were all given one month's hard labour. A tramp was given seven days' hard labour for stealing a roadman's lunch, and Thomas Jones was prosecuted by Francis Gilham, proprietor of the Garibaldi, for threatening behaviour and obscene language.

Henry Larton was constable for Lent in 1878 and George Buckland and William Watkins for East Burnham, and in 1892 Arthur Trimming was appointed for Lent and Thomas Bennett for Town and Wood — ten years later he became parish clerk.

William Swabey had been followed as post master by Henry Style and Charles Ashton; then, in 1864 James Harrison Jarrett began his 40 year term of office. During his time the Post Office passed from strength to strength. In 1864 there were two deliveries and two dispatches to Maidenhead each week day and one on Sunday. There was a Money Order Office and Savings Bank and soon Government Annuities

and Insurance were obtainable. Mr Jarrett also held the office of Deputy Registrar. By this time the Mail coaches had been superseded by the railway, and the telegraph service came in 1877.

Until the closing decades of the century the villagers drew their water from wells, lit their houses with candles or oil lamps and walked through dark streets at night. Then in 1864 the Burnham United Gas Light and Coke Co was formed and Mr Fuller appointed as lighting inspector at a salary of £4 per annum. In 1878, 25 street lamps were erected, furnished with Luff's regulating burners 'to consume 4 cubic feet of gas per hour at a cost of 4s per lamp'.

Owing to pressure from Dr Wilmot who was concerned for the health of his patients, the Burnham, Hitcham and Dorney Waterworks was formed in 1892 to supply safe drinking water for the village, by sinking a well deep into the chalk at a cost of £1,500. Directors of the Company included Captain Farwell, Augustus Terry, H. Mellett, G.J. Williams, G. Wethered, Frederick Cleare and Dr Wilmot, with Alfred Heald as secretary. This company supplied the village with piped water, and also stand pipes by the Crispin Inn and at the bottom of the High Street.

A scheme was also under way for surface drainage in the village. The upper part of Burnham '. . . as far as the fall of ground will allow up to the Britwell Road, and on the Dropmore Road from the house occupied by William Blackman . . .' was to be drained into Opendale Pit, which had already been giving trouble because of the accumulation of water. Mr Trumper was given a contract to collect house refuse, calling from house to house once a week with his horse and cart, for £20 a year.

George Ivey the blacksmith became Captain of the Fire Brigade in 1883. He put £20 in the Post Office towards a new engine and collected subscriptions until £223 had been raised for a Merryweather manual pump pulled by two horses. To accommodate this the Fire House had to be extended and John Merry Roberts, who owned an adjoining cottage, allowed part of it to be incorporated to give the extra space.

There were 12 volunteer firemen then, and in December they were called to a 'great fire' at Windsor where, with their new engine and 780 feet of hose, they outshone all other brigades. A few years later however, when called to a fire at Cleare's farm, there were red faces all round when the Engine House key could not be found, and they were beaten to the scene by the rival hand pump from the Britannia Foundry. Rules for the Captain issued in 1892 tell us 'The Engine is not to be taken out of the Parish without the consent of the overseers except in case of fire' and 'The engine is to be tried with Wet Practice four times annually. 1s per man per practice shall be allowed by the overseers'. Practice took place at the village pond. In 1895, when Harry Baldwin was Captain, he was paid £10 a year. When fire broke out a messenger ran through the streets blowing a whistle to call the men.

Albert and Sarah Kent became Master and Mistress of the village school or the Mixed School as it was called in 1888. Several extensions were made to bring it up to standard to receive a government grant for maintenance. Cloakrooms had to be provided, and a room for cookery — previously Mr Hanbury had allowed them use of a room in the Mission Hall. The Infant School needed a new classroom and, as a

temporary measure, the Mistress's bedroom was used, while poor Miss Charlotte Childers had to sleep elsewhere — the managers did pay the rent of a room for her. Later the School House was enlarged and she was able to return. The money for the extension had to be raised by extra subscriptions, from those who had already paid an annual amount to maintain the voluntary status of the school. In the 1890s Mr Kent held evening classes in Commercial Arithmetic and Bookkeeping, the Vicar also held classes for 'lads and young men' and there were lectures at the Mission Hall on Insect Pests, and Horticulture. In 1900 Mr W. Hyde held classes in Pitman's Shorthand, which were attended by several ladies, including Miss Tollemache, who gained their first certificates.

School Managers at this time were W.M. Bayley, Henry Cleare, Capt Farwell, P. Headington, J.M. Roberts, R.F. Rumsey, C.G. Dawson-Smith, G.S. Willes, A.E. Wilmot and Thomas Jones who, as secretary, did the weekly job of checking and signing the registers. In July 1893 they appealed to the parents through the Parish Magazine to send their children to school regularly. When the children had to pay their School Pence the Managers returned half the fee to those who achieved a full week's attendance, and consequently attendances improved. Now that education was free, parents had nothing to gain by sending them. Some boys were persistently absent on Tuesday and Thursday afternoons, for Geography and Drawing classes — perhaps not regarded as useful subjects for earning a living. A concert, however, was always popular. In March 1896 A. Wilkins, E. Bovington and C. Trimming performed *Urchins We* and, in a cantata *Babes in the Wood,* T.R. Kent (son of the headmaster) and H. Hawkins as the babes, played their parts with great success.

Measures were in hand to improve the health of the people. Scarlet fever and diphtheria were common; measles and influenza were still dangerous diseases. Schools were closed when these reached epidemic proportions, and the rooms sprayed with cyllin before the re-opening. A scarlet fever epidemic started one November but, as Dr Wilmot was away, there was no medical authority to close it, and 400 attendances had to be made made before the closure was allowed. Ringworm was also a frequent complaint among the children. In 1882 the Vestry minutes recorded that 'a trained nurse is available to relieve the sickness among us' and there were frequent attempts to arrange for a nurse to be permanently on hand. At last in November 1892, a Committee was appointed under the capable direction of Lady Louisa Fortescue and Miss Tollemache, to raise funds for a nurse for Burnham and Dropmore. Dr Wilmot was appointed Medical Officer of Health and Public Vaccinator in 1883, and in the same year the Burnham Provident Dispensary was started. It was designed to help 'those above the Pauper Class who are therefore not entitled to Parish Order' (ie free treatment as provided by the Poor Laws) 'yet find difficulty in providing themselves and their family with medicine'. A few years later Burnham Provident Medical Club began, to help people to save for their needs in time of illness — an early kind of Health Insurance.

In 1907 Parish Councillors were elected by ballot and Miss Katharine Tollemache, local benefactor extraordinary, became the first woman councillor, remaining one until 1920. She died in 1921, at the age of 84.

At the turn of the century Burnham had a parcel post and an Express delivery. The Post Office was incorporated in Sydney Rhys-Williams' chemist's shop in 1907 and he advertised 'Telephone Express Delivery Office.' When Charles Burnell opened a stationer's shop in 1939 where Cleare's farm had been, the Post Office moved there and the sorting office was behind. It remained there until the early 1960s.

The United Telephone Company of Cannon Street, London had been given permission to erect poles and overhead wires along the Bath Road in 1888, but it was twenty years later when the National Telephone Company took a 21 year lease on Richmond House in Britwell Road and opened Burnham's first Exchange. This was a manual exchange operated by two maiden ladies, the Misses Walker. There were 17 subscribers, including Edward Clifton-Brown, Holland Buckley, Major Munro, R.H. Cleare, Barr & Sons Nurserymen, and the International Tea Company's Stores. In 1913 the Company was taken over by the Post Office and in the late 1920s a new exchange was built at Northend. Doris Stannard, Edie Davidson, and Joy Taylor had joined the Misses Walker by this time, and worked at the Exchange until 1933.

Changes came to the village school when Mr Kent became ill in the spring of 1908 and died shortly afterwards, having for many years had an uphill struggle against large classes and inadequate staffing. Mrs Kent continued to teach until 1920 and their son Reg worked as a pupil-teacher under the next Master, Francis Buck — a young man of progressive ideas who drilled his pupils physically and mentally in true military style. They stood to attention at the first whistle, came to their positions 'at the double', and were regularly inspected for neatness and cleanliness. They were encouraged to join the Children's National Guild of Courtesy and write essays on 'The Evils resulting from the Misuse of Alcohol'. Attendances rose to an average of 93 per cent; 2 December 1909 was a great day — 'Perfect attendance at both sessions — the flag was hoisted to celebrate'.

Mr Buck stayed until 1923 with a two year break for war service. During his absence Thomas Doran took over as temporary head. In 1917 Capt Albert Kent, eldest son of the previous headmaster, was awarded the Military Cross for distinguished service in the field. In 1923 Mr Buck left and Mr Doran succeeded him, holding the post for fifteen years until his retirement. He was followed by Charles Griffiths 1939-46, W.G. Arthur 1946-9 and Lloyd Willimott 1949-54.

The Police Station in Stomp Road was built in 1928. The local force consisted of Inspector Neal and three constables. It was customary for recruits to be trained at the local station. A class of four men lived together in one small room containing four beds and a chair. Meals were eaten at the guardroom table and the sergeant's wife did the cooking. The recruits were not allowed to leave the station except for obligatory attendance at church twice on a Sunday, and had to be in bed by 10 pm, when the sergeant would come in to extinguish the spluttering gas-burner. November 1902 was a busy month for the local force. A workman from Britwell Farm discovered the body of a man in a ditch in Burnham Beeches, which proved to be a case of suicide. Later in the month Wrights' grocer's shop was burgled during the night. The family

living above heard nothing, but next morning found the cash box open and £20 in gold missing. The dog in the back yard had been given a large plate of poisoned meat, but fortunately survived.

Special constables were elected in time of need. In the early days this was at election time, and later during the General Strike and the two world wars. Grocer Cecil Collett, who joined the Special Constabulary in 1914 and served for 25 years, remembers about 25 volunteers attached to Burnham Police Station in the 1939-45 War. They patrolled in twos and he was paired with Headmaster Tommy Doran, who lived to be over 90, and with Charlie Small, who was knocked off his bike while on duty, and fatally injured. They had to patrol the Trading Estate, almost choked by the oil burners which gave off a dense smoke to hide the Estate from German bombers.

A new Fire Station, with a bell tower, had been built in 1908. The bell was cast at the Britannia Foundry. Ernest Castle was responsible for ringing the bell, and was paid £5 a year to be in the High Street 24 hours a day. He did however have an assistant, Mrs Norrel, who stood in for him on occasion. It was now decided that an escape ladder was needed — this was also used to test new recruits, who had to climb to the top while the crew raced them up Church Street and back. If they fell off, or gave up, they were no use. The next innovation was a steam fire-engine which arrived at Slough by rail and was pulled home by two horses, accompanied by a cheering crowd.

By 1914 horses were no longer readily available, so then came the motor-engine, a Merryweather BH042 which made Burnham the envy of the neighbourhood. Brigades from Slough, Eton, Uxbridge, Maidenhead, Weybridge and Langley came to watch its first demonstration at the village pond. Painted vermilion with Burnham Fire Brigade in gold letters it would drive out into the High Street with bell ringing, and provided such a shock to one driver that he stopped dead and was hit in the rear and pushed into a shop window. Some time later the firebell was replaced by a rocket but, when in 1936 it landed on a shed occupied by a courting couple, it was taken down and replaced by a siren, and bells in the firemen's houses. When this had to be discontinued during the war, the wives hung white sheets out of the window when the bells went, as all the men worked in or near the High Street. During the war the engine sometimes attended fires in London. Ron Allder, arriving late one day, hung onto the tailboard all the way to Ealing. Another act of gallantry was that of George Hearn, who leapt from the roof of the Priory to test the jumping sheet. The crew were also called to Burnham Beeches when a 'plane came down there, to rescue an airman stuck in a tree.

Others to give long-standing service were village doctors, most of whom lived in Burnham House, practising in the surgery there until the new Health Centre was built. Dr Alfred Wilmot and his son Robert, and Dr Croley, followed in the 1920s by Dr Maxwell Summers, his wife Evelyne, and Dr Harold Jacques, all supported village activities as well as giving a fine medical service. District Nurses Rippon and Frost were regarded as ministering angels, walking or 'cycling miles in all weather until old age obliged them to retire.

ABOVE: Infant School 1928. Back row: Miss Cricture, ?, Bray, L. Watts, ?, V. Boon, ? 3rd row: ?, A. Johnson, Lane, ?, E. Thompson, N. Stabler, C. Keen, J. Stanley. 2nd row: ?, S. Gough, ?, O. Quarterman, G. Blackman, D. Barnshaw. Front row: R. Boon, W. Ruffle, F. Simmons, Smith, G. Webb, M. Lawley, B. Flatt. *(DSB) BELOW: May Day 1931.* P. Poole, D. Blackman, B. Flatt, G. Tindall, ?, D. Watts, ?, ?, ?, ?, J. Collins, R. Goodrham. *(DSB)*

71

ABOVE: Infant School c1927. Back row: Miss Reece, A. Hurdle, G. Handley, Adaway, ?, G. Button. 3rd row: Newell, J. Cox, M. Slater, G. Burrows, J. Harman, P. Potter, ?, B. Poole, J. Tripp. 2nd row: P. Jewitt, O. Rule. L. Williams, ?, J. Collins, E. Hearn. Front row: Burns, J. Poulter, Flatt, Tindall, ?, ?, ?, B. Woodward, P. Gough. *(JH) BELOW: The May Pole 1933.* R. Small, M. Lane, D. Strickland, K. New, D. Keen, E. Lloyd, N. Poulter, G. Tindall, D. Blackman, ?, ?, M. Hughes, A. Williams, R. Millership, M. Bray, E. Lake.

(DSB)

ABOVE: May Queen ceremony 1934. ?, U. Clinton, A. Blackman, B. Thomas, T. Tripp, D. Blackman, B. Springall, G. Deeks, M. Goodrham, L. Adaway, ?, ?. (DSB) CENTRE: Spring Flowers 1934. E. Hearn, ?, B. Brooklin, B. Thomas, B. Ottoway, M. Goodrham, D. Adaway, A. Maynard, D. Blackman. (DSB) LEFT: Cookery class 1908, with Mr Buck, headmaster, and Miss Brooks (later Mrs Rhodes), (EH) and RIGHT: Upper School class c1910. (DD)

73

ABOVE: Upper School class c1911, (DD) and BELOW: Upper School class 1920s. Standing: Mr Doran, ?, H. Bunce, T. Millership, R. Cox, G. Limmer, Mr Crighton. Seated: R. Crumplin, ?, ?, M. Young, O. Stannard, Barlow, ?, G. Blackman. Front row: J. Jones, H. Sparks, C. Totman.

ABOVE: Upper School c1922. Miss Phillips, mistress, Mr Doran, master, and BELOW: Upper School c1920. Back row: Elston, ?, G. Limmer, Bradley, I. Murfitt, Herbert. R. Blackman, ?, Mr Dobson. 3rd row: D. Stannard, ?, V. Hester, ?, ?, V. Stannard, W. Coxhead, N. Winch. 2nd row: J. Haycock, F. Cox, Yates, W. Hawkins, G. Marks, D. Sands, H. Gibbons, G. Stepney. Front row: ?, G. Adaway, ?, W. Burnhams, Dolman, J. Adams, Flatt. (BS)

ABOVE: School team, winners of the Grenfell Shield for football, 1933-34. Standing: Mr Doran, Fred Evans, Alf Burnhams, Ron Collins, Tom Grant, Jim Taylor, Bill Bleines, Mr Waters. Seated: Bill Cyster, Tony Redhead, Steve Lee, Ted Goodrham, Walter Lake, Doug Keen. (JT) BELOW: Boys' football team, 1907. (FJ)

ABOVE: 1932, the year Burnham won six cups in the Inter-school sports. Back row: Audrey New, Fred
Evans, Pat Cashman, Edith Hearn. 3rd row: Mr Doran, Jim Anderson, Bill Saunders, K. Small, Margaret Webb, Mackie Jones, Win
Shervall, Beatrice Tindall, Rene Young, Ron Bleines, Mr Waters. 2nd row: Stan Appleton, Margaret Henson, Miriam King, Eda Hulm, Bill
Cyster, Tom Grant, Peggy Rich, ?, George Bacon. Front row: Bob Evans, Dorothy Brooklin, Ron Chandler, Monica Williams. *(WM)*
BELOW: A patriotic operetta 'Birth of a Union Jack', performed by school children, in aid of the
War Relief Funds 1915.

ABOVE: School Morris Dancers 1924. Standing: Dorothy Jones, George Blackman, Annie Stanton, Dick Lechmore, Olive Stannard, ?, Lottie Hulm, George Adaway, Vera Fisher. Seated: Betty Rich, Eddie Catherall, Eileen Hawkins, George Hester, Grace Walker, Alfred Sands. (OB) CENTRE: School Pageant at the Gore c1921, (BS) and BELOW: Christmas School Concert, 'The Pied Piper', 1957. Back row: Patrick Jinks, Billy West, Linda Millis, Susan Peters, Terry Hearn, Ian Brown, Denis Ventham, David Carey, Pamela Davies, Andrew Rodwell, Edward Rushby, Linda Green, Carol Lay, Linda Parkin, Marilyn Hamilton, Sandra Foley, Billy Lawrence. Front row: Christopher Stevens, Terry Callaghan, David Boshier, Brian Cox. (BS)

LEFT: The Village School in Church Street, 1871-1971; (DH) RIGHT: the School House, rebuilt several feet further west, as it is today, as a private house; CENTRE: Church Street. The house, right, of the Five Bells, was occupied by Mr Kent, headmaster, 1888-1908, (BS) and BELOW: Burnham Gore. The three pairs of cottages on the left formed the original school, built in 1811. George Almond converted it into cottages in 1871.

ABOVE: An artist's impression of the School and School House; (BS) CENTRE LEFT: Hitcham School, built 1859, now 'Cloverdown' a private house, west of the church; BELOW: pupils at the Misses Deverill's school, c1912. This later became 'The Pantry', now 27, High Street. (MEC) RIGHT: Reedham House was a private school in Britwell Road in the 1930s. Part of it is now Penstone Veterinary Surgery, and BELOW: the Infant Convalescent Home, built in Green Lane opposite the Golf Club, in 1920.

ABOVE: An artist's impression of Church Street c1800, with the stocks and cage left and the Market Hall right. The cottages at the end were demolished to make way for the school in 1871; (BS) BELOW: the George Inn, which magistrates found more comfortable for meetings, than the building across the road, built for the purpose. (BS)

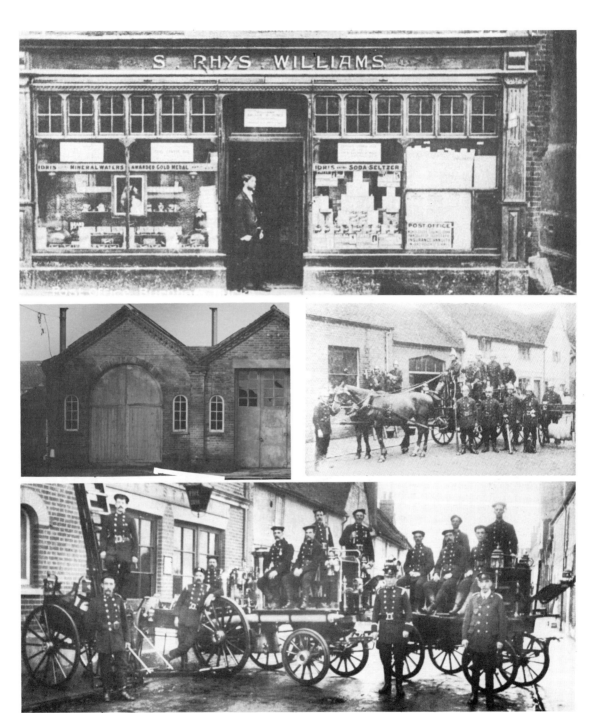

ABOVE: Sydney Rhys-Williams outside his chemist's shop, where he also ran the Post Office from 1905-c1933; (BS) LEFT: the Pumping House at the Water Works in Gore Road, built 1892; RIGHT: the Fire Brigade 1896. Sharp (call boy), Brooklin, Moreton, Bailey, Harry Baldwin (capt), Williams, Stevens, Allder. Foreground: J. Painter, Knight, Lanton, Webb, Cox. (RA) BELOW: The Fire Brigade c1910, with the new steam engine, outside the new station built 1908. Standing, right in the foreground: Harry Baldwin (capt), T. Jones; others include Ernie and Reg Jaycock. (BS)

ABOVE: The Merryweather motor engine c1936. Reg Pemberton, Bev Harrison, Ernie Brooklin, Arthur Sawney (known as John), Harry Baldwin (capt), Ron Allder, ?, ?. (BS) BELOW: Ron Allder, fireman extraordinary, from 1925-1968, at his wedding party at the Swan, 1934. Back row: Reg Pemberton, ?, Tom Herbert, De Ve Webb, Tom Spufford, Ernie Jaycock, Bev Harrison. Front row: Harry Jaycock, Brooklin, Ron Allder, Mrs Allder (nee Hebbes), Harry Baldwin, Fred Flatt. *(LA)*

LEFT: The house built for the District Nurse in 1923, where many a cut knee was patched after school, through the passage by the Fire Station; (BS) ABOVE: tarring Burnham High Street 1909. Second from the left is Jimmy Adams, the well known chimney sweep; (MEC) CENTRE: Burnham House, built c1840. Former home of Dr A. Wilmot, then his son Dr Bob, and later Dr Maxwell Summers, (BS) and BELOW: Burnham Civil Defence Corps, at the Priory c1946. (AE)

TRADERS AND TRANSPORT

Pigot's Directory of 1830 tells us that Burnham as a place of trade was inconsiderable, and possessed nothing of a business-like nature with the exception of two iron foundries. Nonetheless, for those who lived and worked there, like butcher Richard Cleare and shoemaker James Winch, trade flourished and tradesmen were instrumental in running their own small town.

In 1813 cattle, sheep and horses were traded at the annual Fair in Church Street and William Austin, a market gardener, advertised Knight's New Pea at 2s per peck. Richard Boncey's iron foundry at the south end of the High Street, where he made castings and agricultural implements in iron and brass, was well patronised by local gentry and farmers. By 1830 it had been taken over by Benjamin Baldwin and, as Britannia Foundry, was run by his family for 90 years. The other foundry at the top of the High Street was run by John Cutler and later by John Moreton, when it was called Hope Foundry.

Other traders were builder James Webb, blacksmith William Painter, baker Thomas Briginshaw, and nurseryman Joseph Winch; soon to join them were grocer William Bennett, butcher John Hall, carpenter George Almond and corn dealer John Webster.

Between 1820 and 1830 the population increased by 600, to 2,137; at the same time the population of Maidenhead was 945 and Slough consisted of the villages of Upton and Chalvey with a population of 1,052. With the coming of the railways ten years later, these two towns outgrew Burnham, though it also gave impetus to trade and industry in the village.

In the 1830s there were four inns, two butchers, three bakers, two grocers, two saddlers, three blacksmiths, three nurserymen, several builders, carpenters and painters, seven shoemakers (boots were a continual necessity, especially in growing families and on the land) and five tailors and dressmakers, some of whom supplied servants' liveries for the local gentry. The Winch family was prominent in local life with Joseph a nurseryman, John a hurdlemaker, James a shoemaker, Daniel a corn dealer and Charles a clock and watch-maker and bird stuffer.

The Rose Brewery had been leased from Eton College by Thomas Howard at a rent of 13 gallons 2 quarts of wheat or 110 gallons of malt, in 1798. When he relinquished it in 1841 the rent had increased to both the above quantities plus 17s 8d. The Brewery consisted of a brewhouse and a malthouse with two working floors, a malt loft, a barley loft, a kiln and a screening room.

Tollett's stage-coach left the Swan for London at 7am every morning via Stoke Poges, Iver and Hayes. Seats inside cost 7s while those travelling on the roof or in the luggage basket paid 3s 6d. Richard Austin, nurseryman and landlord of the George, ran the carrier's waggon, travelling the same route as the coach on Tuesday and Friday and carrying passengers too, at a cheaper rate. This service was later taken over by James Austin and Giles Tombs who were also farm managers.

Grouped together in Church Street with the Church, market hall, slaughterhouse

and inn, were a butcher, a baker and a maker of straw hats. The other shops were in the High Street; the lower part was called the Parade and the section further up by Cleare's butcher's was later known as the Arcade, and that beyond the crossroads as Northend.

By 1842 the village also had a chemist, William Crisp, a coaldealer, Joseph Wells, and Thomas Williamson had become Registrar of Births and Deaths following the General Registration Act of 1836. In 1844 there were eight beer-retailers besides the inns, James Walker of the Red Lion also being a hairdresser, which probably made having a haircut a convivial occasion.

Haymill was run by John Hillman, whose family served the village there for nearly a century. A brickworks and kiln stood in Breach Field where we now find Lent Rise School and the Chiltern Road estate; a part of the engine house was discovered here recently. Another brickworks was in Lent Field on the site of Milner Road, and the licensing of the Brickmakers' Arms at Lent Green in 1835 bears witness to this local trade.

The Great Western Railway reached Taplow in 1837, crossing Burnham parish south of the village, disrupting farmlands and putting the stage coach out of business. On the credit side it brought railroad workers who provided extra trade for the shopkeepers and inns, employment for local men in gravel extraction and brickmaking, and extra business for the tradesmen who ran flys between the village and the station opposite the Dumb Bell. This station was replaced in 1871-2 by Maidenhead and Taplow Stations respectively, its location marked by the Old Station Inn.

The carrier remained in business; from 1847 William Williams held that role for some 30 years. His waggon went from the Swan twice weekly via Slough to 69 Old Bailey. Edmund Brown had taken over the Rose Brewery, afterwards forming a partnership with Augustus Terry. John Hall at the age of 21 opened the butcher's shop which he ran from 1839 until his death in 1907. William Bennett, forerunner of the family bakery business, started in 1844 as a grocer and slop seller. Thomas Mellett opened a grocery and drapery shop on the top corner of the High Street, south of the Crispin, which his family ran successfully for 55 years.

A second generation of traders was branching out; James Painter became a shoemaker, and William Webster began farming at Dorneywood. John Cutler's family were much in evidence: Joseph and Benjamin were ironmongers and carpenters, Jane a mercer and Clara a dressmaker. When Benjamin died he was sadly missed as a respected tradesman and as a member of both the Yeomanry and Oddfellows.

Most of the High Street buildings were cottages at the turn of the 19th century, but the population, having expanded to about 3,000 by the 1850s with a consequent increase in the number of traders, many were being converted into shops. James Harrison Jarratt, later to fill the role of Postmaster for 40 years, ran a grocery and drapery store. In 1864 he advertised 'Strong whalebone stays at 1s 11½d, good calico at 2¾d a yard, men's flannel shirts 3s 11d, cord and moleskin suits, and

women's stout elastic-sided boots 2s 11d'. Around this time Alfred Heald set up as a chemist and druggist; a gifted musician, he sang in the choir and soon became organist at St Peter's, a post he held for many years. He was agent for the Sun Fire and Life Assurance Company, and for W.A. Gilbey, advertising 'Gin 2s to 2s 10d, rum 2s to 3s, brandy 2s 2d to 5s 6d, and whiskey 2s to 3s a bottle'.

John Cordery had been the village blacksmith for over 20 years and, when he died suddenly in 1863, his wife Jemima, who carried on his trade, disputed Dr Gillam's diagnosis of heart disease. A long legal battle ensued as to whether an overdose of morphine had been carelessly prescribed. Among the jury were his fellow-tradesmen James Webb, Benjamin Baldwin, Thomas Mcllctt, William Bayley, Edmund Brown, James Jarratt and Samuel Cutler.

By 1864 the growing village supported six bakers, including Bennett's, whose shop opposite the New Inn was patronised by the gentry and advertised 'Our bakings are carefully attended to'. Children living in the cottage behind the bakery would fight for the warm bed next to the wall backing on to the oven.

Richard Cleare's family branched out in the 1870s; his sons Henry and George had taken over the butcher's, but George died and Henry moved into farming, passing the butcher's shop to his nephew Frederick William. The eldest son, also Richard, took over the Dumb Bell Inn in 1842, the year of his marriage, and ran it as Cleare's Hotel until his death in 1888.

John Hall had now been an established butcher for nearly 50 years. Delivering meat to Beaconsfield one day he met a runaway horse and cart and, the lane being narrow, was forced to leap over the a hedge to avoid a collision. Besides driving his own cart, John also had a license to let flys.

Advertisements in the Parish Magazine tell us that 'Mr Baldwin at his foundry makes cast iron plates with names, dates, etc, for graves in the churchyard; prices from a few shillings to about 25s', and later 'Having been in the employ of the late John Ball for 25 years and now taken over his business of saddler and harness maker, I desire to continue your kind support . . . signed, John Preston'. Saddlers, harness makers and blacksmiths were vital to village life; blacksmith George Ivey became Captain of the Fire Brigade in 1883 and in the same year Henry Hebbes, corn merchant and coaldealer, took over Haymill. Mr Cleare raised subscriptions to buy a water cart to lay the dust in the High Street which became a great nuisance in dry weather. The cart, which cost £23, was made by Mr Baldwin and operated by the Road Surveyor, Mr Cutler.

Robert Lawley started his family business then as a furniture dealer, and William Lund was a tailor. Both their families eventually became newsagents. By the early 1890s George and John Webster had taken over Brown and Terry's brewery. Jess and Joe Harris worked for the brewery, delivering beer; their brother Alf tells how they used a phonograph on their cart when travelling at night, to make would-be robbers think there were more than two of them. They were also said to have given information about the gentry to the footpads — perhaps in return for their own safe passage.

A printing works was started in Britwell Road in 1891 by William Hyde, secretary of the Rifle and Football Clubs, and it remained in the family for over 50 years. George Almond the builder had bought the old Gore School in 1871, converting it into cottages and adding an extra pair at the northern end; he also built the earlier houses in Almondville. His name is preserved beneath the church floor, where some planks are inscribed 'This piece of flooring was laid by G.W. Almond and Arthur George Hyde, better known as old Joe Hyde, May 17th 1893'. Harry Baldwin joined his family in the iron foundry, taking it over in the early 1900s, together with the Captaincy of the Fire Brigade, in which he had succeeded George Ivey and remained in command for 41 years until 1938. Haymill passed from Henry Hebbes to Stephen Rogers, whose family ran it until its demise in the 1950s.

In the 1890s a man was paid 6d a week to sweep the horse droppings from the High Street before the 8am church service on a Sunday, but changes were on the way with the advent of the steam engine and motor car. Thomas Pritchard advertised traction engines of all kinds for hire in 1895. These early engines were preceded along the roads by a man with a red flag. In 1901 an 11 ton engine from the Dorneywood Kiln Company broke one of its wheels in the High Street, and fell forward, blocking the road and causing great danger to the crowd of sightseers. Messrs Baldwin were sent for and eventually moved it with great difficulty.

The days of the carrier's cart were numbered when Burnham Beeches Station opened in 1903. However, Ernest Castle, fly proprietor, who provided horses to pull the fire engine, seized the opportunity to start a horse and carriage service between the station and the village. The days of the horse were by no means over and John Aldridge started a second saddler's and harness business although one had sufficed the village for the last 50 years. His shop adjoined the Crispin, while the other, Arthur Lloyds, was next to the foundry. Arthur's brother Fred was a blacksmith and shod horses from a small shed next to Rhys-Williams' chemist's, providing an attraction for passers-by in the High Street. Richard Henry Cleare, son of Frederick the butcher, combined the old with the new, being a farrier, general smith, hot and cold water fitter, coal merchant and manager of the water works. His brother, Frederick jnr, lived in the farmhouse in the High Street just below the foundry and opposite the Feathers Inn. He kept small animals in the farmyard behind the house and his cattle in Eight Acres Field. In the early 1900s he started a threshing and rolling contractor's in the Engine House at the junction of Northend and Back Lane (now Fairfield Road), and later moved to Poyle Farm.

'Cycling was the craze in Edwardian England, and Rowland and de Vere Webb (known as Dicky) opened Burnham's first 'cycle shop next to Cleare's coal office. Frederick Bayley had been one of the earlier 'cyclists and owned a bone-shaker with wooden spokes and iron tyres.

Motor vehicles were more frequent and a speed of 10mph was imposed on High Street traffic. The first garage appeared by 1915. Trimming and Company set up in a large house on the corner of Stomp Road and Lent Rise Road with petrol pumps outside. Four years later William Sands, a young man who had come from Ireland in 1903 with Sydney-Richardson Christie-Miller, as his groom and chauffeur, started

up in business on his own. Trained as a mechanic at Rolls Royce in Derby, he rented a barn at Britwell Farm where he sold cans of petrol and bought a car to run as a taxi. By 1920 he moved with his family into the High Street brewery premises and, working hard all hours of the day and night, soon had a flourishing business. In due course two of his sons and a daughter Dorothy who did the book-keeping, joined their father. Robert later ran a second garage at Slough, while Alfred continued to supervise the limited company at the Burnham end until recent years.

Fred Raynor, landlord of the Crispin, owned a Zenith motorbike, the first to be seen in the village, and also bought a 10 seater motor-'bus to take local people on excursions. The early 1900s also saw the advent of the larger grocery stores, Budgen's and the International Tea Company, and Collett's Stores replaced Mellett's. William Collett's son Cecil, who ran the shop till 1956, tells us that when they first came to the village in 1908 a weekly market was still held in Church Street. In the High Street a vendor wearing a top hat covered in fly-papers shouted 'flies, flies catch em alive'; keen gardeners were ever ready with bucket and shovel to collect the horse droppings, and cows, pigs and poultry still wandered through the streets. One day a cow caused havoc in Mr Jones' chemist's shop. Cecil was a certified grocer, having gained his diploma, and worked hard from 7.30am till 7pm Monday to Saturday. Goods arrived in bulk in those days: tea, sugar, cheese and soap came in crates of 1 cwt or more and had to be weighed up and packaged out of hours. Each egg was candled before sale: held up in front of a light to ascertain its freshness by showing up the vacuum. Golden syrup came in casks and one night a cork blew out, and Cecil found the cellar floor two inches deep in syrup next morning. At that time sugar was 2d a pound, tea 1s 2d, cheese 10d, and bacon 1s 4d.

The proximity of Burnham Beeches Station stimulated housing developments to the south of the village, and in Lent Rise, a mainly Victorian development spreading downhill from the hamlet of Lent, James Jarratt's son had opened a grocer's shop in 1903, on the corner of Lent Rise and Nearway (now Eastfield) Roads. About 1912 it was taken over by Wilfred Cornell, by whose name the cross-roads became known; the shop was also a sub post-office. Plevey's butcher's was opposite, just north of the Methodist chapel. Shortly before the first world war Frederick Moon ran a dairy in Milner Road, which later incorporated the post office, and moved in the early 1930s to Eastfield Road, where Miss Glading's haberdashery, Harding's coal office and Charles Williams' baker's were already established.

The development of the Trading Estate in the 1920s provided work for those living in the village and attracted new workers to the locality from considerable distances, including Wales and Scotland. This gave a boost to local trade, and more new shops opened on the southern outskirts of the village. There were many planning applications for houses and bungalows then and many new roads were built, particularly in the area of Haymill Road, Burnham Beeches Station and Cippenham. The first Council houses were now built at Orchardville; the Eton Rural District Council planned to build 66 in Burnham as 'there was no parish more in need of housing than Burnham. Some of the existing houses were not fit for a dog to live in, let alone human beings'.

Harry Baldwin sold his foundry c1917 when it was taken over by Charles Stannard, who ran it together with his brother-in-law Harry Wood and opened an ironmonger's shop next door. Manhole covers marked Wood and Stannard are still to be found. In 1924 a row of old Tudor cottages opposite the foundry were demolished to make way for a row of shops, including Mrs Beane's (later Dorothy Thatcher's) outfitters and Frank Knight's stationer's. New traders in the High Street included bakers Maurice Bennett, Harry Castle and Frank Maybanks, and later Albert Lidstone. Other new arrivals were Bigg's the upholsterers, Millership's shoe repairers, Burnell's stationers and Frost's estate agents.

Ernest Castle had progressed from a fly proprietor to motor proprietor and Strickland's garage was in business behind the George Hotel. At Herbert Lund's 'cycle shop you could hire a bicycle for 6d a half-day and for the same price have a wireless accumulator charged. Hinton's stores was run by the Allen family, who were later also landlords of the Red Lion opposite. Frank and William Haycock were greengrocers in the High Street and Stomp Road, and others followed in the same trade — Stratton's, Collison's, and Stephen Horwood at Lent Rise. John Cox opened a small grocers at Lent Green which later became Thomas Bond's and then Jessie Binfield's. In 1923 Wilfred Cornell applied for a grocer's off-licence at his Lent Rise shop, but this was refused, as the Maypole and the Brickmakers Arms were within a short distance.

The first Thames Valley 'bus service through the village was in operation in 1921. Five years later, Simmonds Brothers started the Reliance Bus Service, with a stop at the bottom of the High Street. The return fare to Slough or Maidenhead was sixpence, and it also linked the village to Burnham Beeches and Taplow Stations.

From 1919, charabancs could be hired but, a few years later, there was a move by the District Council to ban them from roads around the Beeches.

In 1923 George Ashley, a motor driver of Station Cottage, who worked for the company which held the rights to ply for hire at Burnham Beeches Station, assaulted another driver who was trespassing on these rights. He was fined £2 plus one guinea for the doctor. A few weeks previously there was a collision at the Five Points, between a car driver by William Barrett and a motor cycle belonging to John Allder; both vehicles sustained considerable damage. A number of fines were also imposed on 'cyclists for riding without lights — a common misdemeanour then.

By 1931 High Street shops included a bookseller — Mrs Barratt; a photographer — Mr Ferris; Miss Glading's Fancy Repository, and a leathergoods manufactory run by Charles Harper at the Old House (later the Old House Restaurant).

In the early 1940s twenty-five trains a day in each direction ran from Burnham to Paddington, and twelve on Sunday. A first class return was 10s 4d, third class 6s 2d. Thames Valley 'buses ran at 15 minute intervals. The Parish Guide Book tells us that 'practically every trade has one or more representative. It is not at all necessary to go to town for household things'.

Of those in business in the early 1800s five names came down to the 1950s: Almond, builder; Painter, undertaker; Bennett, baker; Hall, butcher; and Cleare, butcher and coal merchant; the last two still here today.

DEALS AND WHEELS

ALFRED J. HEALD,
CHEMIST AND DRUGGIST,
BURNHAM.

AGENT FOR W. & A. GILBEY.
Price Lists on application.

Gin ....from 2/- to 2/10 per bottle
Rum .... „ 2/- „ 3/- „
Brandy .... „ 2/2 „ 5/6 „
Whiskey .... „ 2/1 „ 3/1 „

J. FULLER,
Baker, Corn Dealer, and Mealman,
BURNHAM.

Dinner and other Rolls. Cakes made to order. Fancy Bread
of every description.

RICHARD BUTLER,
Baker, Mealman, &c.,
BURNHAM, BUCKS.

CAKES MADE TO ORDER.
Pure Bread without adulteration.

WILLIAM H. P. FIELD,
(late Thomas R. Chotles,)
TAILOR,
BURNHAM, BUCKS.

LIVERIES MADE TO ORDER.
Black Suits from £4.   Tweed Suits from £2 10s.

*Agent to the United Kingdom Temperance and General Provident
Institution.*

*ABOVE: John Hall, butcher, with his family 1854. John lived to be
90, running his shop for nearly 70 years, (BS) and BELOW:
advertisements in an 1869 Parish Magazine.*

ABOVE: Walter (Wally) Hall left, with his children John and Vera, displaying the Christmas fare, c1900; (BS) LEFT: Arcade House, now Dear's butcher's shop, with a built in boot scraper, remnant of the pre-macadam days, (BS) and RIGHT: Arthur Lloyd's saddlery between the foundry and Cleare's farmhouse, 1907. (BS)

ABOVE: Cecil and Percy Collett, outside their store c1912, (BS) and BELOW: inside Collett's store 1923, where you could buy almost anything; the last shop of its kind to survive in the High Street, till 1956. (MC)

ABOVE: Hinton's hardware shop was opposite Cleare's Coal Office and run by Ernie Allen before he became landlord of the Red Lion; two of his daughters posing, c1909, (BS) and BELOW: the pride of R.H. Cleare's coal yard c1900. (BS)

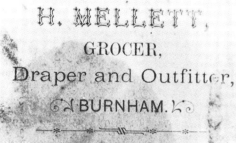

ABOVE LEFT: The International Tea Co, started in Balm's shop c1908, later moving to this store, after Whitely's left, c1935; RIGHT & CENTRE: advertisements in a Parish Magazine, 1904. BELOW: Five minutes' break at Wood and Stannard's iron and brass foundry c1920; Burroughs, Cox, Tom Manning, Johnson, Fred Cox, Francis Stannard, Harry Wood, ?, Len Challis, Charles Stannard, (BS) and RIGHT: manhole covers made at the foundry are still around, some even in Malta.

95

ABOVE: Charles Stannard's family c1920. Standing: Doris, Nora, Elsie, Vera. Seated: Charles, Joan, Francis, Mrs Stannard, Olive, (OB) and LEFT: Charles Stannard, a keen gardener, with his plaque as first life member of the Gardening Society, 1953. (OB) RIGHT: The Westminster Bank, 1911, which opened Wednesday and Friday 11am-2pm.

ABOVE LEFT: Rose Brewery c1890; the archway now leads to Sand's Garage workshop, (BS) and RIGHT: the Old Malt House, leased by Thomas Howard in 1798, burned down in 1982. CENTRE: George Hebbes at his corn shop door, which was next to political HQ in 1930; here, Sir Alfred Knox is on the winning candidate's chair, with old Mr Lawley beside him. BELOW LEFT: Harding's coal cart delivering to the Five Bells, Church Street; their yard was by the railway bridge in Lent Rise Road, (c1915); RIGHT: advertisement for Clark of Lent Rise, in a 1929 parish magazine.

OPPOSITE ABOVE: Tudor Cottage in Church Street, was a shop at the turn of the century, when the Bricklayer's Arms, extreme left, was still there, (BS) and CENTRE: Lent Rise c1915, when Wilfred Cornell had taken over Jarratt's ironmonger's to become grocer and sub-postmaster, while Charles Williams' bakery is further along Nearway Road, now Eastfield; LEFT: Trimming and Co started the first garage in Burnham, at the corner of Stomp and Lent Rise Road, c1915, (KT) and RIGHT: Lent Rise Road looking north, with Trimming's Garage right and Plevey's butcher's (now Lent Rise stores) left, c1922. (JT) ABOVE LEFT: In the doorway c1922, is R.E. Plevey with his son centre, who later ran the timbered butcher's shop on the opposite corner; RIGHT: Lent Rise Dairy in Milner Road c1911, later Moon's Dairy and post office; (GM) CENTRE: in the early 1930s, Fred Moon moved to this site, 3, Eastfield Road; (GM) BELOW LEFT: the only shop at Lent Green, formerly John Cox's in 1924, here Thomas Bond's 1928, and later Jesse Binfield's, in a brick building, (FJ) and RIGHT: Haymill prior to demolition c1958; it stood opposite the railway at the south end of Burnham Lane, where lads swam in the stream 60 years ago. (BS)

99

ABOVE: A group of brickmakers c1880, and CENTRE: the Kiln, still in Brickfield Lane, where bones and potsherds were found in 1936. BELOW & OPPOSITE: Advertisements of High Street traders, in Parish Magazines 1929.

*BELOW LEFT: The **Daisy May** traction engine, (BS) and RIGHT: F.W. Cleare's agricultural machinery works, at North End c1927; driver, Steve Cox. (BS)*

ABOVE: Dumb Bell Bridge Station, as it was from 1838-1871, where the Old Station Inn now stands, (BS) and CENTRE: originally the Dumb Bell Hotel, opposite the old railway station (Richard Cleare, farmer, ran it from 1842-1888) it then reverted to the name Dumb Bell. (MEC) BELOW: The Catherall family stayed at the Mile House in 1911, visiting Burnham Beeches in the Inn's landau, driven by Ben and Trevor Owen, sons of the landlord. (DSB)

ABOVE LEFT: Frank Maybank's new delivery van, c1935; (BS)
CENTRE & BELOW: Edwin Johnson of Station Garage, Taplow,
*with **The Taplow Queen**, which he used for excursions in the 1920s.*
(AE) ABOVE RIGHT: Fred Raynor, landlord of the Crispin, on his
Zenith motorbike, c1915, (FJ) and CENTRE: W.J. Sands at the
wheel of Mr Ingpen's car, c1930. (BS)

ABOVE: At the Brickworks c1925: Mr Carter, William Wheeler, ?, 'Wizzle' Wheeler, ?. (BA) BELOW: Cleare's Hotel proprietor Richard, with his wife Ann, brother Henry, and OPPOSITE LEFT: sisters Jane and Amelia. (MEC) RIGHT: Hall's butcher's shop c1955, showing the initials of the founder and his son, on the eaves; (JH) CENTRE: Cleare's lorries loading up with coal, at the railway siding, by the bridge in Lent Rise Road, (FBC) and BELOW: Richard, Clara, Florence and Fred Cleare, c1906, grandchildren of Richard Cleare, butcher, who came to Burnham in 1814. (MEC)

FUN AND GAMES

There was not much to celebrate or enjoy in the early 1800s when the Napoleonic Wars were drawing to a close, bringing years of depression. Only two of the three annual Hiring Fairs took place then and, by 1830, only the October event continued. Ostensibly serious occasions, for trading in live stock and the hiring of humans as servants, the fairs provided an excuse for festive holidays, for many the event of the year, with visiting minstrels and the like.

Local hostelries played their part in providing entertainment; the Crispin, Swan, Five Bells and the George were those listed before 1822. As the stage coach stop, the Swan run by Daniel Long no doubt provided evening jollities for passengers, while the George offered a venue for such things as the Annual Melon Feast. In 1816, you could show one melon free and have dinner served at 2pm for 4s. At that price, it was an occasion for the gardeners of the gentry, not the labouring poor, who spent what little they had in the tap room. In 1825, landlord T. Lawrence at the Mile House sold gin at 1s 8d, rum at 2s 6d and beer at 3d a pint, with cheese at 9p a pound. The population was increasing and, between 1830 and 1840, licences were granted to the Alma and Grenville Arms, where Neville Court is now, the Bricklayers' Arms in Church Street, the Red Lion at the top, the Boot in the centre and the Feathers at the bottom of the High Street, all on the west side.

Others were trying to offer alternatives to beer swilling and in 1828 Benjamin Baldwin became a pioneer of the sporting scene by raising a cricket team from among his employees. They played matches in the meadow behind his foundry against other traders on early closing day, while encouragement was given to those who had learned to read at school, when a Reading Room and Library opened in the High Street in 1853. Run by Mr Field the tailor, one could borrow a calico covered book for ½d, to be washed and returned clean, and penny readings were available for those unable to afford newspapers, which cost 6d each.

Imbibing seems to have been the favourite pastime however, since the Rose and Crown opened next to the Swan in 1856, and the Garibaldi (under that name) in 1862, making 12 pubs in all, plus numerous beer retailers and the New Inn yet to come; no wonder temperance workers became active.

Determined to liven things up, the local tradesmen revived Whit-Monday as a social occasion in 1862. Shops closed at mid-day and a cricket match, followed by sports and a tea for the elderly, all took place on the Gore. The sports included a greasy pole, running blindfold with a wheelbarrow, donkey racing, eating rolls and treacle, gingling, etc, with clothing tickets for prizes. The occasion was so successful that next year the gentry came, this time at Hitcham Park, loaned by Richard Webster, where Samuel Christie-Miller opened the show and the Ladies Grenville and Sitwell joined in the fun with the working classes.

Cricket had become so popular by 1870 that rules were drafted for the Burnham Cricket Club, which competed with neighbouring clubs.

The subscription was 10s and the first elected committee consisted of W. Carter, Rev L. Sweet, G. Almond, F. Cleare, H. Mellett, A. Terry, H. Hebbes and J. Hall (Secretary).

A few years later, football had become the rage, and the Burnham Club was the second to be formed in the County, in 1878. Games were played in Baldwin's Meadow, behind the Foundry, and entrance through a wicker gate in Dawes East path cost 2d. Early members were mostly tradesmen, including H. Baldwin, G. Allder, W. Briginshaw, W. Hyde, W. Sarsons, J. Tilbury, C. Jarrett and Arthur Jaycock, whose job it was to mark the pitch and put up the goal posts.

In the same year, a large part of the Dropmore Estate was purchased by Sir Henry Peek, who then sold it to the London County Council. It became Burnham Beeches, providing an area of beauty for the benefit of the public. Consisting largely of trees, with open spaces ideal for picnics, it was soon used as an 'outing' venue by the villagers, and by others pursuing unlawful hobbies. One man had more than he bargained for, with 14 days' hard labour for stealing moss.

By 1883, the social scene was developing fast. The Workmen's Reading Room had moved to larger premises in Church Street where, at the inauguration, the Hanbury's 'Blythewood Band' entertained. Here also concerts, lectures and dinners were held, with Mrs Payne from the Swan as caterer. A Bagatelle craze had hit the town, when matches were played at the Reading Room, in the pubs and even in the Beech Tree Coffee Tavern, a venue for teetotallers, where the Hon Mrs Boyle was patroness. She furnished and extended it, hired rooms to temperance movements, sold soup to the poor at 1d a pint and on one occasion gave tea to a touring German Band she met playing in the High Street.

As a further sign of growing affluence that year 'cycling had become the 'in thing'. Within a few years, Burnham Club events, held in Baldwins meadow, attracted competitors from as far afield as London. In 1866, prizes were presented by the Duchess of Marlborough, when W. Briginshaw and H. Timberlake did well for Burnham in the two mile handicap.

Children were not forgotten and from 1883 were given an annual school outing, while those who went to Sunday School got two. After a church service, Mr Cleare's decorated coal carts conveyed them either to Cliveden, Taplow Court, Hedsor Court or the Beeches, where games and sports were organised, while Mr Terry, the brewer, provided tea. The curate 'cycled beside the cart on the way home, calling for cheers, when passing the home of a benefactor.

The ancient custom of Maying provided a bit of pocket money for enterprising children. Carrying wooden hoops decorated with ribbons, they called at the large houses, singing, 'Here we come a-Maying, through the meadow straying', and requesting ribbon for garlanding, were usually given pennies.

To celebrate Queen Victoria's Golden Jubilee in 1887, the day began with a Thanksgiving Service at 11.0am, followed by sports in Mr Cleare's meadow (now Minniecroft housing estate) — a splendid affair which the local notables attended, giving generous prizes, while Mr Cleare maintained a mounted patrol. The following day, wearing special rosettes, 100 children walked to Taplow Station, then by train to Slough, where stands by the orphan's asylum (now Licensed Victuallers School)

gave them a grand view. Bread and butter and cake, left over from the previous day, with water to drink, kept them happy until the Royal party's train arrived. At last, horse drawn carriages conveying Her Majesty, the Russian Prince, Princess Christian and the Duke of Edinburgh passed by, while the children sang the National Anthem.

Although the Annual Fair was not used to hire servants after 1884, it continued as a social function. Elsie Winch, an old Burnham resident, recorded her childhood memories of the fair in the 1890s, when it was held in Church Street and the High Street. People from surrounding parishes would arrive early and enterprising cottagers opened their doors to offer a welcome meal. For 6d, one could have roast pork, potatoes and cabbage, with apple pie to follow, while a pewter mug of beer cost 1d extra. As a customer put down his horn-handled knife and fork, another would be ready to take his place. Schoolchildren were given a holiday and pennies by the gentry, to spend on roundabouts, gingerbread, trinkets or the traditional 'fair rock'. An old gypsy claimed her longevity was due to beer, tobacco and this rock, which she had been making for 87 years. When the fair was over, not one piece of litter was left by the gypsies.

For those who could afford it, a nine hole golf course, with a wooden pavilion, was laid out in 1891, on land adjoining Green Lane and the Beeches, with subscriptions of £2 for men, £1 for ladies. Local lads were soon supplementing family incomes, acting as caddies, while learning a thing or two about the game. Caddies came in three classes: 10-12 yr olds got 7d a round, 12-15s got 10d, while the older, experienced lads, were paid 1s, with 4d extra for lunch if they worked all day. This was spent at the caddy master's shop, where one could buy a bottle of pop and 10 biscuits for 2d.

The attraction of displaying horticultural prowess had caught on by 1892, when the first major show took place in Baldwin's meadow. Subsequently, it was held at Britwell Court, Miss Tollemache's house, Benteleigh and finally at the Priory, which became the regular venue until 1940. Some classes were for the 'professionals', gardeners of the gentry, while others were for 'amateurs', the working class. In 1901 Burnham and Hitcham Horticultural Society was formed with Miss Tollemache as secretary. The Annual Show gradually became the most important social event, incorporating arts, crafts, flower, fruit, fur, feather and vegetable classes, in which everyone participated, while John Hall and his son Wally provided a pig to be bowled for and side shows kept everyone amused. In those days, the marquees and prize money were given by the gentry.

Meanwhile, as always, quick to take up new activities, Burnham Rifle Club, the second to be formed in the country, had begun in 1899. At first, practice took place in Baldwin's meadow, then Capt Farwell, the President, offered a range at the Priory, H. Baldwin was captain, with R.H. Cleare, J. Allder, A. & W. Hyde, W. Fuller, J. Foulk, H. Swaney and J. Painter among the early members who paid 5s to join and 4d to practise for ammunition. Not to be outdone, in 1901 the Misses Slater, Cleare, Allder, Belcher, Hinton, Wright and A. & E. Lawley, applied for membership and were accepted, a Remington rifle costing 18s 4d purchased for their exclusive use.

However, chauvinism reared its head the following year, when the ladies were told they must have 12 members and only 8 applied. The club became affiliated to Bisley, competing there on many occasions, and within a few years had moved to the range in Aldbourne Road, where it remains today.

With an increased number of social activities, the Workmen's Reading Room had become inadequate. In return for permission to divert the main road past the front door at Britwell Court, Sydney Richardson Christie-Miller founded a new Workmen's Institute in 1903. It contained a 1,000 volume library, billiard and card rooms and an entertainment hall to seat 200. On opening day, the founder said he wanted to bring to the poor man something of the privileges of the rich.

That same year saw the forerunner of 'Hospital Sunday', an annual event which was to take place for the next 50 years. Initiated by the Church, the whole parish took part in a grand parade through decorated streets. The choir, local brass bands and organisations, some on decorated carts, made their way from Church Street to Lent Green, while collection boxes were passed among spectators. The parade ended with a service opposite the Pheasant Pub and a collection to help maintain local hospitals. Dr Maxwell Summers became a legendary figure in later years, leading the parade on horseback, wearing exotic costumes.

Baden-Powell's first great Rally to introduce Scouting to the nation in 1909 caught the imagination of Mr Walter, who formed a troop in Burnham the same year, with six boys. Using Bennett's Barn in Chapel Street as HQ, they camped in Mr Hanbury's field. The following year a Burnham Troop was officially registered, with A. Merritt, Scoutmaster, assisted by H. Kent and two patrols. By 1916, Rev I.K. Jones, affectionately called 'Ikey', had set up a gymnasium at the Mission Hall and also ran the Scouts there. John Butler recalls that as leader of the Owls, his patrol included Douglas and John Nott, Howard Rix, Wells, Johnson and Savage. They travelled by army lorry to camp at West Wittering, practised field duties on the vicarage lawn and impressed the village by becoming county champions, and winning a cup at the Aylesbury Jamboree.

At the village school, sports and social activities were endorsed. In 1905 they won the Grenfell Elementary School Shield for football, a feat not to be repeated until 25 years later, when Reg Kent, one of the original players, was a referee. In 1910 the Vicar allowed the vicarage pond to be drained and cleaned, for use as a school swimming pool, and Morris Dancing displays and concerts were performed at the school.

Encouraged to contribute to the war effort, in 1915 they put on a patriotic show called Birth of a Union Jack, to raise war relief funds and, in 1917, gathered 1,230 lbs of blackberries to make jam for the troops.

About 1905 football and cricket matches were played on the present football ground at the Gore, where hessian was draped along the hedge to stop folk peering through. A wooden pavilion, presented by Ernest Teitkens, was built, and one bucket of hot water supplied for 22 players to wash in after the match.

Edward Clifton-Brown, who later purchased the football field and presented it to the village as a sports ground, also donated the Village Hall, built opposite the

waterworks in Gore Road, in 1912. Run by volunteers, it had a stage and dressing rooms, providing a social venue for all the new activities.

These activities were at least keeping folk out of the pubs, since by then the Bricklayer's Arms, the Rose and Crown and the Boot had closed down, along with some of the beer retailers. At the Grenville Arms, Boaz Gohm sold sweets and milk at the back, 'Chunky' Knight at the Feathers was also a postman and boot repairer, rooms were let at the Swan and the George, while the Alma ran a darts club, the Buffs met at the Crispin and the New Inn provided a meeting place for the local ferreters. No doubt these extra activities helped them to make a better living.

The family of W.H. Williams of Bredwood were all public spirited and, in 1914, two of his daughters started the Girl Guides. The company consisted mainly of daughters of local notables, ie Fuller, Clifton-Brown, Cleare, Sands and Christie-Miller, who let them use the laundry at Britwell Court (now St Anselm's) as their headquarters. By 1917 the company was registered officially as 1st Burnham, with Ruth Williams (Captain), and 36 guides drawn from the whole parish.

Entertainment reaching Burnham from the outside world was mostly confined to travelling theatrical companies, who gave performances in Bennett's barn, opposite the Chapel in Chapel Street. The audience sat on wooden planks and the shows were referred to locally as the '2d gaff'. However, by 1915, Burnham boasted its own electric cinema. Ernest Jarratt, son of the erstwhile Postmaster, fitted out a barn in Lincoln Hatch Lane, known by the local wags as 'Plush's Barn'. Cyril Cox worked the projector while Miss Frost and later Gertie Murkett rendered appropriate piano music according to the film being shown. For a penny, one could watch silent films of Charlie Chaplin, Buster Keaton and the like; not that the audience was silent, far from it, and Mr Jarrett frequently had to keep order amid the catcalls and stamping feet, when the film broke. When it closed in 1922, a live theatre replaced it for a few years, and until recently, the title 'Burnham Electric Theatre', could be seen at the front of the building (now a warehouse), with a board at the side window saying, 'Pay Here', giving 1920 admission prices.

Bursts of musical activity came and went. At the turn of the century, Burnham had its own brass band for a couple of years. Around 1912, a choir flourished at the Mission Hall in which Marjory Collett, her sister and two brothers sang. It must have been good because Mr Starkey from St George's Chapel, came to conduct it. Then after the first war, Vicar Percy Nott and his four children, all gifted musicians, formed an orchestra and choral society, giving concerts at the Village Hall.

The Rifle Club continued to flourish, winning the Bucks County Challenge Cup in 1919. Edward Clifton-Brown was their president and by then they were travelling to Bisley in Edwin Johnson's coach, *The Taplow Queen.* Hockey and Tennis Clubs were active in 1920, when tennis courts were in the field by 'piggy path' and John Hall secretary to both. Two years later, having arisen from within the Rifle Club, Burnham Bowls Club was formed, a green and wooden pavilion built for them on the Aldbourne Road site.

A mania for golf had gripped the poor as well as the rich after years of caddying. The present Club House had replaced the wooden one, the course was extended to

18 holes and the Club formed into a limited company in 1909. Jim Isaac, who started caddying at 10 and playing at 13, recalls how Mr Chesney the 'pro' and sometimes members would lend or give clubs to the lads with which to practise. By 1920, an Artisans Club was formed. £1 of the guinea fee went to the Parent Club as green fees and 1s into their own fund. Sir Courtauld Thomson, their first president, took an interest in caddies, giving them prizes each year for the best kept teeth. The lads would clean their teeth with a mixture of salt and soot, hoping to win either 5s, 3s 6d or 1s 6d prize money. Horses stopped pulling the mowers once the engine arrived and, when the last horse died in 1930, it was buried near the eighth hole with a sentimental ceremony.

The football field closed during the first war. When presented to the village as a sportsground in 1920, it became the venue for football, cricket, tennis and athletics. In 1921, with Dr Croly, President and Charles Holloway, Secretary, Burnham District and Hitcham United Services Athletic Association started, under AAA rules. Held on Whit-Monday, the sports attracted participants from far afield, but Burnhams' A.J. Woodley, who won the Astor Challenge Cup for the 1 mile 'cycle race in 1914, when racing stopped, won it again in 1921. The next year he joined W. Bunce, P. Stannett and W. Merry to represent Burnham in the open one mile flat handicap.

By 1927, the Guides had moved to the Village Hall, where they acquitted themselves well in Rallies. From 1914 daughters of W.J. Sands, Gwen, Molly, Jean, Dorothy, Margaret and Sheila, became almost a legend in guiding and ranger activities. The village Hall became the ARP HQ, so a permanent home, 'a timber town' hut for the Guides, was found in 1939 and put on the site now occupied by the Jennery Lane car park.

The Scouts, meanwhile, had been moved around, first to the Priory, then to a hut of their own by the Infant School. The second war caused disruptions to Burnham and Hitcham Troops. In exchange for summer camps and gang shows, they did ARP duties and ran errands for the wounded at Cliveden Hospital. After the war, Bert Bovington became Scout Master with Arthur Grout, Ray Portsmouth and David Guire as assistants and the Burnham and Hitcham Troops amalgamated, moving later to the present Almond Road site.

The war caused changes in other organisations. As they had done in the first war, women rushed to join the Rifle Club, to be in a better position to protect their homes in the event of invasion, while the Rangers joined the Civil Defence Corps en bloc, carrying out such duties as ambulance drivers and first aid officers.

The meaning of the phrase in the guide motto 'to help other people at all times', reached its zenith in Burnham in 1948. Sisters Nancy and Gill Treleaven organised a Guide Company and Brownie Pack in the Rheumatic Ward at Cliveden Hospital, where handicapped children spent many years of their lives. With the help of staff and others, they gave these children fun, and a sense of belonging to the outside world, with which they could compete, and in fact they won many competitions. This act typified the spirit of Burnham. We may lose sight of it periodically, yet it is always there in time of need.

THE SOCIAL SCENE

LEFT: Regulars outside the Pheasant, sharing a jar with landlord Joseph Portway c1940; RIGHT: a far cry from its days as the New Inn, where local ferreters met on Sundays, (BS) and BELOW: the Crispin, where the Buffs held their meetings. (BS)

112

ABOVE LEFT: Bearing witness to Lord Grenville as a neighbour, the Grenville Arms stood in Bustle Row, where Neville Court is now; c1950. (By courtesy of the Windsor Slough & Eton Express) RIGHT: The Feathers, where 'Chunky' Knight was the landlord and E. Clifton-Brown's chauffeur lived next door, c1928; (BS) BELOW LEFT: the Garibaldi, c1925, (BS) and RIGHT: Ernest Allen, landlord of the Red Lion until it was replaced, on the same site, by the new pub, c1940, seen here with his wife and daughters, c1935. (BS)

LEFT: Challenge Cup for the One Mile 'Cycle Race, presented by Lord Astor in 1907. Winner that year was H. Eaton, then successively, D.V. Webb, S. Pemberton, A.D. Webb, A. Hazeldine, H. Bailey, J. Benson, A.J. Woodley. (EH) RIGHT: Advertising the Annual Melon Feast, at the George, 1816. (By courtesy of the Windsor Slough & Eton Express). BELOW: Sports day at the Gore 1922, with A. Hyde, J. Hall, C. Holloway and Dr Croly, watching form. (BS)

ABOVE: *Winners of the South Bucks & East Berks Junior League and the Wycombe Cup, 1897-98.* Standing: A. Oliver, F. Cleare, A. Wright. W. Hyde (sec), R. Wingrove, S. Hawkins, W. Tutte. Seated: D. Gregory, G. Adaway, R.H. Cleare (capt), H. Buckland, J. Harrison, *(BFC)* and LEFT: *celebrating in the garden behind Cleare's butcher's shop, 1898. (MEC) BELOW: Winners of the Bucks Minor Cup 1902.* Standing: S. Mitchell, Burnhams, Limmer, P. Bennett, C. Bennett, B. Hinton, T. Blackman, J. Carter, D. Hinton. Seated: Quarterman, G. Hancock, H. Britton, J. Adaway, A. Butler. *(BS)*

ABOVE: Champions of the South Bucks & E. Berks Junior League 1905. Standing: A. Adaway, J. Carter, W. Hyde (sec), R.H. Cleare, J. Tilbury. Seated: A. Butler, J. Shipton, Serls, H. Britton, A. Kent, B. Hinton, J. Fryer (capt); (BS) LEFT: at the new pavilion, Gore Road, 1908, including Ned Wheeler, 'Wizzle' Wheeler, 'Ringo' Adaway and Bill Dealy. (BFC) RIGHT: Winners of the South Bucks & E. Berks Junior League 1920. Standing: ?, Carter, ?, F. Evans, ?, ?, R.H. Cleare, A. Hyde. Seated: ?, ?, ?, E. Goodrham, G. Strickland. (BFC)

LEFT: Cricket Club members 1928. Back row: C. Holloway, T. Pearce, V. Lund, J. Welsh, B. Janes. Front row: G. Coombes, J. Bellairs, C. Holloway (sen), W. Piggot, Col. Parsons. T. Eason. (BCC) RIGHT: Cricket team c1932. Standing: M. Dolman, V. Pearce. W. Hutchins, J. Bellairs, M. Pierce, S. Williams, E. Appleton. Seated: J. Isherwood, G. Stobard, T. Piggot, W. Baker, G. Williams, R. Sands, T. Strickland. (BCC) BELOW: The Annual Top Hat Cricket Match, held on Cippenham Green, c1940. (BS)

LEFT: 1952 Cricket Team. *Standing: G. Williams, A. Brown, K. Herrington, G. Hedge, A. Dickens, L. Hawkins. Seated: A. Ratcliffe, J. Bartlett, A. McKinnon, A. Grout, W. Gough, E. Starks, G. Lines.* (BCC) *RIGHT: Burnham & District Rifle Club badge; (BRC) CENTRE: the Aldbourne Road firing range, when the Rifle Club moved there in 1907, (BRC) and BELOW: bringing the spoils home, after a successful day at Bisley:* V. Trimming, H. Trimming, W. Fuller, H. Haycock, H. Wood, C. Stannard, ?, H. Lloyd, ?, ?, B. Painter, G. Lloyd, outside the foundry 1919. *(OB) ABOVE: Camp Inspection at Cookham Dean 1910. Burnham, Taplow and Hitcham Scouts, (JH) and BELOW: Scout Troop c1911, outside their HQ, the barn in Lincoln Hatch Lane, which later became the cinema.* Seated on the obsolete manual Fire Engine, are, back row: Ernie Marshall, Harry Cox, Tom Brooklin, Frank South, John Clark. Front row: Fred Knight, Trevor Owen, Bill Turner, ?, 'Whacker' Sawney, George Brooklin. Standing: Alf Hatch, Cyril Cox, 'Maggie' Wheeler, Edward Carter (Scoutmaster). *(CC)*

ABOVE: Scouts doing their thing at the Priory, 1921: D. Nott, ?, Sawyer, ?, E. Hammond, J. Nott, Howard, ?, ?, T. Wilson, G. Limmer, G. Adaway. *(GL) BELOW: The first Guide Company 1917:* Back row: ?, A. Walker, ?, V. Adaway, K. Moon, ?, F. Barnshaw, H. Reynolds, R. Winch, C. Watts. 3rd row: R. Hyde, ?, ?, V. Nott, D. Foster, M. Bradley, ?, ?, ?, 2nd row: ?, V. Christie-Miller, M. Cleare, P. Williams, M. Fuller, R. Williams, N. Williams, R. Clifton-Brown; J. Fuller, P. Arden, M. Clark. Front row: G. Sands, R. Christie-Miller, D. Williams, O. Moon, K. Clark, I. Webb. *(GS) OPPOSITE ABOVE: 1922 Guides:* Second row: E. Gibbons, B. Nott, P. Williams, R. Clifton-Brown, F. Dennis, G. Sands. Front row: R. Nott, ?, M. Sands, ?, D. Blackman, ?. *(KL) LEFT: 1st Burnham Guides at West Hay camp 1935; (NT) RIGHT: Successful bowlers at Windsor Castle 1937:* ?, A. Brett, H. Wood, W. Haycock, W. Eyles. *(BBC) BELOW: Rangers, guides and brownies, at the opening ceremony of the new 'timber town' HQ, 1939: front row includes, Miss Binnie, Mrs Bruce-Gardine, Molly Sands and Nancy Treleaven. (EP)*

ABOVE: Bowls Club members c1935, outside the early wooden pavilion, in Aldbourne Road.
Standing: T. Pearce, ?, ?, ?, Goulder, V. Trimming, ?, H. Trimming, ?, ?, ?, ?. Seated: F. Haycock, T. White, Eyles, Col. Samualson (Pres), G.
Boon, A. Brett, Alexander. *(KT) LEFT: Members of the Tennis Club c1920: ?, J. Hall, ?, ?, V. Hall, ?. (MC)*
RIGHT: Ladies Tennis Club 1923: ?, Doreen Cleare, Hilda Cleare, Marjorie Collett, Vera Hall.
(JH) BELOW: Tennis Club Party at the Gore, c1920: Front row: ?, Doreen Cleare, Margaret
Cleare, Vera Hall, ?, ?, Marjorie Collett, John Hall, ?, ?, Wally Hall. (BS)

LEFT: Burnham Golf Club House, built 1909; RIGHT: the Working Men's Institute, built 1903; (BS) CENTRE: Burnham Artisans Golf Club, 1922, (BS) and BELOW: the Alma darts team 1932. (BS)

OPPOSITE ABOVE: **The Gondoliers,** by the Dramatic Society, at the Village Hall, 1938; (KT)
LEFT: Brownies at Lent Green in the 1923 Hospital Parade; (MC) RIGHT: 1923 Hospital Parade
in Britwell Road, (MC) and BELOW: Rev Wildman taking the service at Lent Green, at the end of a
Bell's Parade 1951, with Dr Summers dressed as an Arab. (By courtesy of the Windsor Slough &
Eton Express). ABOVE: The Women's Pleasant Hour Club, ready for an outing, c1920: ?, Mrs Oliver,
Mrs Norrel, ?, Mrs Ostrich, Mrs Adaway, ?, ?, Mrs Brown, Mrs Walker, Mr Alexander, ?, ?, Mrs Brooklin, Mrs Burnhams, ?, Mrs Stingmore,
?. (PC) BELOW: party in 1948, for youth club members who 'came of age' during the war. Standing: Bob
Small, Bob Millership, Ken Trimming, Chas. Griffiths, Don Blackman, Ted Lake, Gerald Gough, Alan Parrett. Seated: Jack Pemberton,
Geoff Parrett, Edna Hearn, Muriel Derrick, Anice Williams, Tony Watts, Desmond Keen. (EP)

EPILOGUE

The 1950s, a time of comparative stability, when the two Church schools were still adequate, when Burnham House surgery and a district nurse could meet the medical needs of the village and the Council Rooms over the Fire Station housed the local library, seemed an appropriate period in which to cease this narrative.

Since then much has happened in and around the village, altering people's lives and to some extent, the landscape. Several open spaces have disappeared, one to accommodate a Health Centre, Day Centre, Youth Club, two schools and a housing estate. The Vicarage Meadow has been swallowed up by Lent Green Lane housing estate, which surrounds the pond, and the Precincts and St Peter's Close cover the old vicarage garden and a recreation ground.

In the 1960s the Priory was sold for office use and much of the grounds purchased by the Parish Council, who removed the northern boundary wall. This improved the aspect from the High Street, giving the effect of a spacious village green, with 18 acres of landscaped parkland in which a new recreation centre (Burnham Park Hall), the Congregational (now United Reformed) Church, the Library and War Memorial now stand.

A large piece of land, which in earlier times formed part of the Britwell Court Estate, is now a residential area, hived off from Burnham as the new Britwell Parish.

Eight new schools have been built and all the large properties formerly owned by wealthy families are now used as offices, educational centres, hotels, flats etc.

Slough Trading Estate has grown larger, bringing more employment, and the M4 motorway, in conjunction with the railway, has made Burnham even more popular as a commuter zone. Consequently the village has expanded as a residential area and the increase in motor vehicles gave rise to the need for one-way traffic in the High Street and other roads.

To most people, the High Street and its environs are still 'the village'. We speak of going up, or down, to the village to shop or go to the Library, Village Hall, Health Centre or Church. So it remains the centre of many people's daily lives. Similarly the social and cultural life which began in the Reading Room, Mission Hall, inns and schools is today centred on Burnham Park and the Secondary School, which accommodates the ever-flourishing WEA and Adult Education activities.

The High Street is now a conservation area, ensuring listed buildings there will not suffer the same fate as the 16th century Market Hall, and closely controlled planning agreements make sure that new buildings blend well with the old.

Already, there is sufficient material here for another book, and our young readers should be encouraged to realise that today's events create tomorrow's history and need recording.

SOURCES

Burnham, Bucks. *An Historical Sketch* by W.H. Williams, (1925).

Burnham C of E Schools' Log Books.

Bucks County Record Office.

Bucks Constabulary Centenary.

Burnham Tithe Apportionment Map and Schedule, (1839).

Burnham's Fire Brigade by Patrick Carty, (1975).

Census Records.

Commissioners' Report on the Poor Law (Burnham), (1834).

Dictionary of National Biography.

First Stop Maidenhead. (Early years of the GWR) by Matthew Wells.

History and Antiquities of the County of Bucks, Vol III, by Lipscombe, (1847).

History and Topography of Buckinghamshire by Sheahan, (1861).

History of Huntercombe Manor by G.F. Thomas, (1965).

Kelly's Directories 1847-1939.

Lyson's *Magna Britannia,* (1806).

Memoirs of Cecil Collett, (1972).

Musson and Craven's Directory, (1853).

Non-conformity comes to Burnham by David Hayns, (1964).

Notes for a History of Burnham by A. H. Packe, (1963).

Parish Council Minutes.

Parish Magazines.

Parochial Church Council Minutes.

Parish Registers.

Pigot's Directories 1830-1844.

Report of the Commissioners (Charities) Vol 25, (1832).

Royal Commission on Historical Monuments, Bucks (South), Vol I 1909-1912.

The Methodist Church at Lent Rise by Hilary P. Evans, (1976).

The Parish Church of St Peter, Burnham by Roy E. Almond, (1961).

The Precious Blood (A History of Burnham Abbey) by T.W.E. Roche, (1966).

The Slough Observer.

The Victoria County History (Buckinghamshire) Vol III, (1905).

The Windsor, Slough and Eton Express.

To and Fro, (History of the postal service of Maidenhead) by J.W. Brooks, (1981).

Vestry Minutes.

INDEX

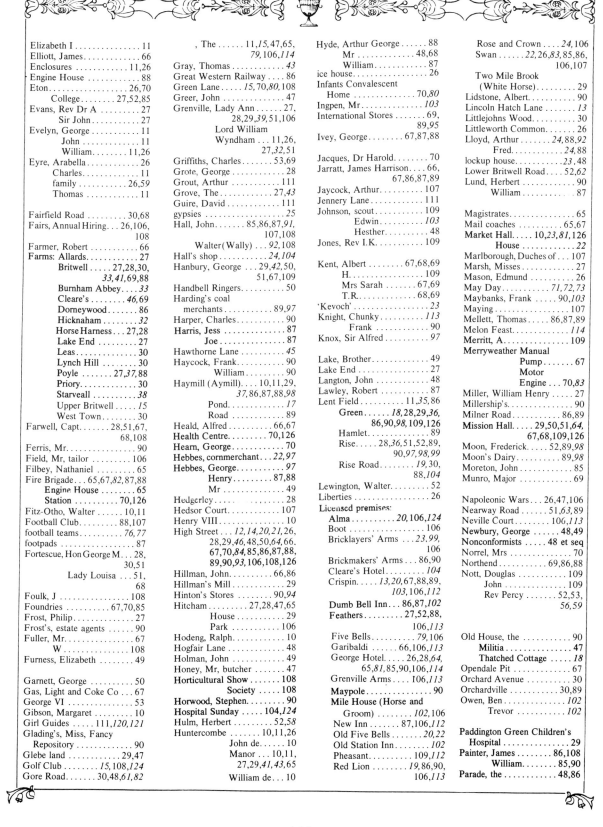

ENDPAPERS: FRONT — *A tracing from Field's map of the Parish of Burnham, c1781; (DW) BACK — the Burnham area c1840, as shown on an early Ordnance Survey 1" to 1 mile map, enlarged to 2½" to one mile. (ME)*

SUBSCRIBERS

Presentation Copies

1 Burnham Parish Council
2 South Buckinghamshire District Council
3 Buckinghamshire County Council
4 Burnham Branch, Buckinghamshire County Library
5 Farnham Common Branch, Buckinghamshire County Library

6 Dorothy Blackman
7 Daphne Chevous
8 Mervyn Eden
9 Anthony Packe
10 Oliver Spencer
11 Burnham Historians
12 Clive & Carolyn Birch
13 E.R. Fryer
14 C.E. Winkless
15 Mrs Barbara A. Reed
16 Mrs Lorna M. Kemp
17 Mrs D.M. Pike
18 Mrs Rita Jane Learwood-Griffiths
19 Mrs Hilary P. Evans
20 Mrs M.M. Day
21 Mrs I.C. Williams
22 Mrs Rosemary Swallow
23 Mrs M.B. Chantler
24 N. Belson
25 Frank L. Jackson
26 G. Hearn
27 Mrs I. Parker
28 L.J. Thorpe
29 Mrs W. Hopgood
30 Mrs S.V. Hart
31 Mrs R.M. Maynard
32 Mrs Prince
33 Leslie & Mildred Tyrrell
34 Stanley & Lena Butler
35 May Stawicki
36 Roberta Ann Heap
37 H.C. Lawrence
38 Michael Dilley
39 Victoria & Albert Museum
40 P.J. Sorbie
41 G.W. Day
42 J.M. Hooker
43 J.A. Anderson
44 I.R. Spillett
45 Mrs A. Metson
46 Mrs Pam May
47 Mrs Voirrey Paesler
48 Mrs S.W. Palmer
49 Mrs Yvonne Isherwood
50 Margaret Kelsey
51 David Crowley
52 Leslie Heffernon
53 Mrs E. Buckley
54 David H. Gayton
55 L. Hester
56 Mrs M. Mount
57 F.A. Yenton
58 Mrs N. Alexander
59 Mrs V. Cox
60 Mrs Lynne Riddle
61 Miss Marjorie L. Collett
62 Mrs M. Scholtz
63 Mrs B. Walker
64 Miss Doreen Strafford

65 K.F. Redhead
66 Mr & Mrs R. Sales
67 Mrs Karen Harding
68 A.H. Lund
69 J.D. Stabler
70 Donald Stevens
71 Mrs J. Bunce
72 R.D. Forsyth
73 I.V. Hawthorne
74 Mrs H.C. Breeze
75 Miss B.M. Kennett
76 Miss J. Robertson
77 Mrs N.C. Rhodes
78 Mrs M. Scharff
79 Mrs Ray Farmer
80 Neil Pomroy
81 Mrs M. Swallow
82 Mrs D.A. Grant
83 L. Hester
84 Mrs J. Lane
85 Mrs R. Holmes
86 Mrs M. Pardue
87 Mrs D. Stearnes
88 Mrs B.J. Pickford
89 A.E. Blackmun
90 Peter Hughes
91 Mrs D.G. Norman
92 J.E. Daniels
93 Mr & Mrs J. Bentley
94 Mrs F.R. Biggs
95 Mrs V. Bucknell
96 D. Haynes
97 Trevor Woodward
98 Graham Woodward
99 Kenneth Robinson
100 Mrs Kerry Hiscock
101 Mrs C. Fisher
102 Mrs M.E.A. Lewis
103 Mrs Diane Martin
104 D.A. Willmot
105 Mr Hirons
106 Mrs Carol Tidy
107 R.G. Lee
108 Mrs D.I. Strickland
109 Mrs P. Badnell
110 Mrs P. Naylor
111 Mrs Mary Catling
112 Mrs A.L. Dottson
113 L.H. Eastgate
114 D.G. Newcomb
115 B.A. Kinnon
116 Our Lady of Peace Middle School, Burnham
117 B.F. Flatt
118 Mrs J. Dyer
119 K.M. Hawthorn
120 J.N.T. Adcock

121 Mrs S. Wyatt
122 Mrs A.J. Prince
123 G.H. Limmer
124 Mrs M. Streatfield
125 Mrs H.G. Smith
126 Mrs S.E. Davie
127 Mr & Mrs P. Illingworth
128 D.D. Miller
129 John M. Smith
130 Mrs D.M.M. Moore
131 H. Sawney
132 J. Lloyd
133 Gerald Higgins
134 Mrs D. Richards
135 Mrs Bertha M. Stevens
136 G.J. Sawney
137 A.W. Dye
138 J.T.H. Jackson
139 Mrs M.E. Hillier
140 Mrs M. Carter
141 Mrs E. Harris
142 Mrs Grace E. Giles
143 R.D. Elliott
144 E. Campbell
145 Mrs H.M. Budd
146 R.B. Thorpe
147 C.R. Ford
148 Mrs B. Heron
149 Mrs M. Scott
150 L.F. Highsted
151 Miss E. Upson
152 Miss M. Cleare
153 M. Green
154 Mrs J. Fidler
155 Mrs J. Cooper
156 Mrs Patterson
157 Mrs L. Allder
158 L. Smith
159 Mrs S.M. Paget
160 C.E. Cox
161 Norman Webb
162 R.H. Jackson
163 Mrs A.D. Elliot
164 Peter Ballinger
165 Mrs E.A. Alder
166 Mrs J .Horton
167 Tracy Anne Rodwell
168 Mr & Mrs K. & B. Shackleton
169 Mrs J. Hunter
170 D.King
171 Wm C. West
172 Louise Caspall
173 Brian Butterly
174 Malcolm Clark
175 Elizabeth Clark

176 M.E. Itter
177 H.L. Warner
178 Sheila John
179 Edward Sammes
180 Mrs Ann Taylor
181 Jill Townsend
182 Luke Williamson
183 Mrs Hilda Wagstaff
184 Barbara Ann Francis
185 Hilary Jean Knott
186 Elizabeth Karen Ball
187 Mr & Mrs K.J. Trimming
188 Diane Armstrong
189 Iris Bovington
190 Robisons of
192 Burnham
193 Margaret Adaway
194 Linda Dobbs
195 Norman Langford
196 Doreen Wootton
197 Joan Doughty
198 Joan Haley
199 Brian Charles Hughes
200 David & Pauline Howes
201 Paul Sherriff
202 Pamela Joan Fletcher
203 David Jeffreys
204 Mrs A.A. Denton
205 R.E. Humphries
206 M.P. Moore
207 M.A. Joy
208 Paulette Jultia
209 Gene Anne Nicholson
210 Miss H.M. Collins
211 R.A.A. Blackman
212 Mr & Mrs. A. Mildren
213 Mr & Mrs Gerald V. Lines
214 Mr & Mrs T. Tripp
215 C.E. Dyte
216 Margaret Bridgeman
217 C.J. Lloyd
218
219 J.G. Carr
220
221 R. Eastham
222 R.A. Hooper
223 Mrs Molly Willcox
224 Eric John Smith
225 John Miles
226 M.F.G. Howell
227 Miss D.G. Clark
228 Mrs Cecil Lilley
229 Mr & Mrs. A.G. Heming
230 Miss D. Bennett
231 John Collier
232 R.C. White
233 E. Cooper
234 Raymond Harding
235 Mr & Mrs M.J. Heming
236 Mr & Mrs P.G. Hill
237 Suzanne M. Blackman

238 Donald L. Blackman
239 D.G. Tricker
240 Gordon S. Planner
241 Mr & Mrs Alfred Sands
242 Mrs Nicola Thomas
243 Miss Dorothy Sands
244
246 Mrs G.M. Harris
247 Joan Handley
248
249 H.S.V. Aldridge
250 Martin Albertini
251 Howard Albertini
252 Nigel Albertini
253 Stephen G. Salter
254 Colin Francis Rowe
255 Phyllis Rowe
256 Mr & Mrs G.G. Salter
257 Ann E.T. Hathaway
258 L.N. Reynolds
259
260 Edith Mitchell
261 D.G. Lidstone
262 Mrs G. Halley
263 Mrs J.R. Kinnon
264 J.D. Cameron
265 Mrs M. Wells
266 J.D. Ware
267 Frank T. Seear
268 T. Jackman
269 Miss J. Barnett
270 W.A. Wood
271 Michael Boxall
272 G.H. Akerman
273 Michael & Hilary Rice
274 Michael J. Hutchinson
275 Anne H. Hutchinson
276 Paul J. Anderson
277 R. Nicholls
278 B. Grove
279 J.G. Latimer
280 Jean Stanger
281 Mrs M. Hargest
282 Valerie Speake
283 W.J. Crimmer
284 Ian Page
285 A. Boon
286 Trevor Hunwicks
287 Mrs N.C. Rhodes
288 Mrs F. Green
289 Mrs Pamela Winn
290 Ian & Mary Dainton
291 Ronald Edward David Potter
292 D.M.N. Scott
293 Doris Aldridge
294 B.M. Wells
295 P.R. Silverthorne
296 E. Gosling
297 B. Spires
298 Arthur Fryer
299 P.W. Payne
300 M. Gibbs
301 Mr & Mrs A. McKinnon

302 Gareth & Suzanne Chevous
303 Jonathan Chevous
304 Mrs Esme Smith
305 Raymond George Cox
306 G.S. Blackwell
307 Jean M. Binnie
308 Mrs P. Vaughan
309 Mr & Mrs G.J. Lund
310 Charles Bellamy
311 Miss M.L. Martin
312 Miss E. Coles
313 R.J. Sands
314 Betty Watts
315 Nigel Watts
316 Patricia Willis
317 Miss E.M. Green
318 D.B. Pinniger
319 Brenda Gray
320 J. Jaycock
321 Simone Davis
322 Daniel Davis
323 N.K. Catliff
324 Evelyn M. Holloway
325 A.J. Broomfield
326 Mrs J. Dunham
327 Mrs A. Bingham
328 Gwen Goodship-Patience
329 Mrs M. Haskell
330 Miss Frances Haskell
331 Caroline Gillies
332 Eric Clark
333 J.M. Mutley
334 Miss A. Alder
335 Bryan & Susie Galan
336 Mrs Linda Wright
337 Mrs Sheila King
338 Eric Chant
339 Pleasance L. Winter
340 G.P. Herbert
341 Mrs S. Painter
342 Mrs Sigthora G. Lloyd
343 Mrs G. Skinner
344 Mrs Joan M. Alderman
345 John R. Weaver
346 David R. Lewis
347 Enis W. Putley
348 D.F. Drake
349 Priory County Middle School, Slough
350 The Wellard Family
351 Mrs G.Hughes
352 Karen Bowes
353 John Peplow
354 Buckinghamshire
393 County Library
394 Mrs N. Price
395 Mrs Linda Deer
396 Rev Peter Judd
397 F. Taxis
398 Michael James Watts
399 Raymond C. Worrall
400 Greta Butler
401 Sydney Dixon
402 Mrs S.M. Bridger
403 Miss G.M. Waters

404 The Nashdom Shop, Burnham
405 W. Akers
406 Miss B.R. Jerrard
407 Mrs J.G. Bland
408 Joyce E. May
409 Mrs E.M. Horton
410 Mrs H.M. Page
411 David Jefferson
412 Mrs H.M. Page
413 Gwen M. Lister
414 Mr & Mrs A.O. Watts
415 W.D. Beaufoy
416 Jack Leonard Jeffery
417 Mrs F.B. Cleare
418 Mrs P.A. Hollins
419 Norman S.T. Chambers
420 R.E. Clark
421 Patricia M. Brining
422 Desmond Keen
423 Mr & Mrs M. Taylor
424 Oliver Watts
425 A. F. Watson
426 Lent Rise School, Burnham
427
428 Mrs J. Willams
429 Mrs D. Hyde
430 Mike & Chris Smith
431 Gladys Evelyn Burrows
432 Mrs Doris Manktelow
433 Mr & Mrs J. Baker
434 Mrs Vernon Hunt
435 David Hayns
436 Bunce Bros
437 (Burnham) Ltd
438 Linda Stainthorpe
439 E.L. Taylor
440 D. Griffiths
441 E.F.J. Perkins
442 Mrs I. Zetie
443 Mrs J. Elsbury
444 Mrs H.J. McGuinness
445 Brian Eric Schoth
446 Connie Macgregor
447 Mrs B. Lightowler
448 Vera Sharpe
449 G.W. Limmer
450 Mrs M.E. Rance
451 Dennis Goch
452 Mrs M. Harris
453 Mrs Anne Othen
454 Miss Caroline Othen
455 Keith & Anne Tildesley
456 Margaret E. Ward
457 Kenneth McInnes
458 J.E. Houlgrave
459 Peter Edward Barrett
460 Rosemary Zorza
461 Geoff & Edna Parrett
462 Edith Baldrey
463 J.E. Smith
464 Dr E. Clive Rouse
465 W.J.M. Greer
466 Mr & Mrs A.H. Bryson

467 Humphrey Bryson
468 C.P. Barnard
469
470 Andrew Hodge
471 Anne & David Young
472 Mr & Mrs V.E. Shuker
473 Roger Platt & Partners, Burnham
474 Florence Maud Coulson
475 Ian Thomas Coulson
476 Alan Coulson
477 Arnold Coulson
478 Jo Armitage
479 Graham Paul Thatcher
480 R.H. Cleare & Co Ltd, Burnham
481 Buers Wine Bar, Burnham
482 James Edwin Petts
483 A.C. Frost & Co, Burnham
484 Mrs N. Grellier
485 Morris Hedge
486 Mrs M.J. Moore
487 Annie B. Evans
488 Helga & Ossie Hanfling
489 Pat & Brian Smith
490 Edward James Pecover
491 Ronald William Rumney Clark
492 N.S. Perks
493 Barry & Geraldine Veal
494 Burnham Rifle & Pistol Club
495 R.E. Almond
496 Malcolm P. Cook
497 A.M. Cawte
498 Jacqui Orchard
499 Lesley Jones
500 Roger Bush
501 Hauptschule Daun
502 Jeremy Saywell
503 D.R. Pepler
504 V.R. West
505 D. Brocklebank
506 Mrs Penelope Dangerfield
507 Antony Sheehy
508 Colin LeMesurier
509 Gordon Campbell
510 Wayne Fitzsimmons
511 Maurice Burnett
512 Gerard Burnett
513 Mr Hulm
514 Burnham County Secondary School

Remaining Names Unlisted: